MY SILENT
REALM

KRUTI MARUTHI RAM

INDIA · SINGAPORE · MALAYSIA

ISBN
Paperback 979-8-89724-299-3
Hardcase 979-8-89744-669-8

Dedication

When it comes to dedication I strongly dedicate this book to my playhome teacher and second mother Sharada miss.
She is indeed a wonderful teacher who has inspired me to the core holistically.

Foreword

'Kruthi' means creation and her parents named her futuristically, hoping she will create something truly worthy. And she has not disappointed them either with her collection of poems, hundred poems have been compiled here but I am sure that she must have written more.

I have known her since her student days and found her to be quiet and engrossed in her own world. Perhaps it was her poetic world which was very own private space, her creative space, a realm of solace to vent out her pent up emotions. She has also strictly stuck to rhyme-rhythm structure. Few poems which I liked are: Flirting with deathly God, Memorable Mistakes and Swami Vivekananda. Kruthi's devotion towards Lord Hanuman is visible in many poems dedicated to her favourite God which she has told in her preface was a sub-conscious part of her growing up years. It is heart-warming to know that she has strong spiritual leanings though young age, and this perhaps empowers her to stride amidst strife. She is an optimistic poet, most of her poems motivate others to move on despite life's ups and downs.

I wish Kruthi the best in all her future endeavours, praying that she hones her creative instincts to create more poems and nurture her literary instincts.

Dr.Mekhala Venkatesh

Associate Professor & Research Guide, Department of English,

Coordinator- GENESIS (Gender Sensitization Cell, JAIN (Deemed-to-be) University

Member- K.S.Narasimhaswamy, Department of Kannada and Culture, Government of Karnataka

Contents

Acknowledgements

About my Ardent Father

At home my father Dr. R. Maruthi ram is the sole inspiration for my spiritual and motivational poetry. He by-hearted 200 to 300 DVG Mankutimmana kaggas. He is popular as sadhguru of our house. Yes has lived so well that I and we siblings cannot pinpoint at his single mistake. So true to his conscious he has lived. Truly he is a very inspiring father. He is a super kannada poet too. He has launched 4-5 kannada poetry books. He is an awesome singer and super tabla player. He used to sing male version bhavageetha song and I and my sister female version of bhavageetha songs. During my early childhood he used to sing kannada lullaby sutti horalaladiru matte hata hoodadiru song almost every day. Without this lullaby there is no day that I have slept without. He is fortunately blest with a wonderful god gifted voice. I call him encyclopedia of our house and all his friends call him a guru even today. In his realm he is was and will be famous father for knowledge. If at all I am a little bit spiritual its all his foundation to spirituality in me. Before we kids were born he had bought books on how to nurture babies and kids and had read them all before we were born. Actually in houses mothers sing lullaby to their kids but here in my house its my father who used to sing lullabies and slowly drive us to sound sleep. We used to sing the lullabies with him and slowly slowly would sleep. This is how I slept everyday. During childhood he was the one who gave us bath, iron our uniform and clean our canvas shoes until the filth is gone. He is a super inspirational father.

About my Super Mother Rekha

She was a great devotee of hanuman diety. She during my early childhood she had made me byheart all the hanuman songs and mantras. Which ever vegetable my father and me used to bring home she used to cook very delicious food out of it. Her cooking enslaved all of us. She used to stich frocks for me and my sister. She was a super veena player who had won many medals and prizes and gave concerts for the skill, super skill in veena. She was a gold medalist in psychology and won scholarship during her PUC and graduation. And my grand father used to give secretly money just for her to go to cinema etc. Inspite of she being a merited student my grand father discouraged her for masters in psychology as he wanted her to marry and settle in life as marriage responsibility was on his head. But fortunately her husband my father stood by her side and she did MBA after marriage in finance so that she will get increments and can support the family economically better. The taste of the food she cooks is alive in my tongue even today. Renowned for unmatchable cooking skills she was known for japa. Even till date I my brother, sister and my father chant hanuman chalisa now we know it byheart already is all her teaching. In every room there is a small picture of meditative hanuman in a photo frame. Though she is a working women name anything she knows where it is in the house. Her signature is seen everywhere in the house. From stiching the clothes to cooking she did all things by herself. My father used to say how to live etc etc but my mother without a saying a word. She has innumerably impacted me hugely is all I say. She was a ruling lioness and my father a ruling lion at home. But every Saturday they used to take us to hanuman and ganesh temple without fail. I used to wonder and was surprised this lion and lioness at my home my parents bowing down to monkey god hanuman and elephant god ganesh diety. Looking at this I decided if I live I have to live like this hanuman and ganesh diety. Slowly slowly my objective of my life became so strong that I wanted to live like hanuman diety and ganesh diety. This thought became very strong in my life. During my childhood I was not much focused by as I grew I became firm to live like hanuman diety and ganesh diety. Living like hanuman and ganesh dieties became my dream and mission of my life. Silently without saying a word my parents had framed my vision n mission of my life. My mother was the one who instilled the devotional lessons and leadership lessons since my early childhood. As I grew up my temptation and focus to live like hanuman diety and ganesh diety increased and became firm. My father used to inspire me to read new story books, swami Vivekananda works, aurbindo's books, shiv khera and badukalu kaliyiri books of guru's etc etc. During my childhood and adolescence and during my college days, I hardly used to study my academic text books rather loved to read bhagavat geeta and poetry books of great poets like William wordsworth, Charles dickens, swami Vivekananda, aurbindo etc. Lots of books other than text books I have studied during my college days and graduation. Outcome of it is my poetry and phrases. If at all I am a voracious reader today its my father's foundation of education to love study. Even now my father has taken some Sanskrit competitive exams. Its his basement to study which made me take interest in study. Even today he reads a lots of yogic books. Like crazy. Since I was inclined to study my mother used to get me a lots of books of study. I had a lot of inclination towards spirituality as my father used to take me to spiritual discourses in gokhale institutes and town hall of swami parthasarathi etc. Near my house there were temples where scholars used to come to give speeches where my father used to take me to. Its was here where my father casually sowed the seeds of spirituality in me.

About my Favourite Grand Mother Susheelamma and my Grand Father Rama Swamy

Though my parents were both working to support the family was a need, I have never missed the love care affection of my mother in the form of my grand mother n blessings and fatherly affection of my grand father. My grand father rama swami tatha used to make me sit on his shoulders and drop me to play home near my house and bring me back from playhome safely. He was very spiritual and was born on ganesh chaturthi. He used to sing classical kannada songs n I used to dance to it in my own wacky manner during my childhood. He was a kannada poet and writer and an author. If at all I am writing its because of his strong and inspirational lessons and strong study foundation of my grand father in my house. My grand mother was a super cook. She used to wait near my house gate till we came home and used to feed us hot hot ragi and rice onion rotis. Sometimes she used to be famous for kai tuttu oota also with wacky stories of animals and birds which used to be so interesting to us we used to listen to those stories with mouth open. Then she used to black mail us if we eat only she will continue the kaituttu oota and shall not continue the story. She used to wait in gate till we came and we used to go in with shoes she used to pull our socks, we used to throw the uniform but she was hell-bent on teaching discipline which we never followed. Then serve us hot ragi and rice onion rotis and with abundant of ghee upon. We used to relish all her roti and onion dishes even today I can recall its taste its alive in my tongue. Her cooking truly enslaved us to the core. My grand father retired govt kannada teacher used to have bananas which he used to cut one banana into five n feed us to we grand children. Even today I eat bananas I remember this incident. No I love you and I miss you they never said but their entire life was we grand children such they have lived. My grand father was a foodie yogi. He used to practice shirshasana at the centre without the help of anybody and pranayama very intentionally. He used to take tutions to my house servent's kids free of cost. He also used to teach devotional songs to the kids near my house and to the kids of his barber. He was very disciplined in his life, have food timely and an extreamely foody. He used to ask his wife, my grand mother to cook delicious food all the time. Such he has lived.

1. The Ineffable Tomorrow

Hey you are, a very famous day which never came,

In your name, in your name, people spoil life's game,

And if I forget your power, you will put me to shame-

If at all you win for god's sake, whom am I to blame;

Hey you are a super eight lettered word is all by name,

I aim to know your worth in every place even at hame-

I truly respect you 'oh tomorrow!' even if I am on fame,

If at all we are ignorant about you
we will surely suffer in shame,

When I valued you and planned my life's
journey all the difficulties I overcame,

I am mesmerised by your competence
'oh tomorrow' you are a bright flame-

With all the glimmer of hope to sadhana
you are an open sesame,

Once I respect you on a regular basis an achiever I became!

You belong to ruler ie King's realm
oh tomorrow so is your game.

Never you are on defame, you are always on high fame,

Hey, so is all your game 'oh tomorrow', so is all your game.

Meaning:-

1. Hame:- a Scots word for home.

2. Open sesame:- something that makes it very easy to achieve
    a particular thing.

2. Rules for Inducement!!!

Truely enjoy, rejoice the very legacy of the enlightenment!

Don't dwell upon or be circumscribed
by other's mere comment,

Simply let your equanimity and patience just, just augment,

Hie work upon the heart dreamt dreams
in every single moment;

When you are happily working smart
with all the encouragement!

Apacingly you will reach your goal with all the excitement;

You stay upon the success ladder forever
with an entire establishment!

But when hindrances are on you fight
it out with high commitment;

Pulverise the very hurdles chill out is
my steadfast statement!!!

Defeating them is not as easy as it's
a big negation department,

There is no inquisitive perky thrill without
excitement & enjoyment,

When we are the strongest, there is no space for the
very bewilderment,

There is no tree, no birds and no life without super
involvement!!!

Life is all inclusive, every time you hied towards excellence & naturally comes achievement!

Just with courage and hopes on lets face life is my humble pronouncement,

Accepting and seeing things the way it is, is but a nice mantra for inducement!!!

Meaning:-

1. *Legacy:-bequest, gift*

2. *Rejoice:-a happy feeling*

3. *Circumscribe:-be under your limits*

4. *Dwell:-unhappily think upon*

5. *Augment:-increase*

6. *Hie:-Quickly*

7. *Apace:-swiftly, quickly*

8. *Establishment:-a permanent stay*

9. *Hindrance:-an obstacle*

10. *Bewilderment:-being perplexed and confused*

11. *Inclusive:-containing as a part of the whole*

12. *Inducement:-encouragement*

3. Lead Life Joyfully

Entire life is itself a purpose you realize ably;

Out-bursting totally in gaily,

Life is beautiful not ugly,

Face this life super boldly;

Experiencing the life gladly,

Don't draw conclusions finally;

Respect your mother nation promptly,

But for devotion be godly;

Give life to every job joyfully,

Be your own mistake finder rapidly;

This life is a joyful journey so enjoy rightly,

You be that awakened & enlightened soul cheerfully.

Meaning:-

1. *Ably:- skillfully*

2. *Gaily:- in a cheerful or light-hearted way.*

4. Life is All a Play!

Dont let not your will power wither away,

Face the difficulties don't run far far away,

Do exterminate all your confusion is all I say;

Let your knowledge & wisdom outreach the bay!

Such you inspire all on high end fame you do stay,

For universal well-being you meditate, don't stray;

Alarm yourself strongly such that you don't lazily delay,

All our entire life is god's super play;

Entire life is just almighty's cosmic play;

Decimate from yourself all the inner decay;

Such you glow that you ignite light in every way,

When the intensity of hurdles is high why astray?

Even before you die all the hidden talent you display,

Oh the joyful one you rejoice that every day is a holiday!

When the mother nation has protected
you so you mustn't betray,

And when success knocks your door
hey you let open that doorway.

Meaning:-

1. Stray:- separated from the group or target.

2. Bay:- a broad inlet of the sea where the land curves inwards.

3. *Astray:- away from the correct path or direction.*

4. *Betray:- expose (one's country, a group, or a person) to danger by treacherously giving information to an enemy.*

5. Today's Learn

Be highly popular for playfulness & frivolity,

Let there be no space for imbecility;

Sell your wit to its entirety,

Outwit the wisest in reality,

Ignite in all the light of possibility,

Wit matters not brawn is the actuality;

Eradicate negativity & double your positivity;

When haziness occurs, finetune until clarity;

Teach the lessons of unity in diversity,

Strongly meditate on the universal diety;

When success arrives stay not in vanity,

And completely obliterate all the cecity.

Meaning:-

1. Frivolity:- lack of seriousness; light-heartedness.

2. Imbecility:- of being extremely stupid.

3. Entirety:- the whole of something.

4. Reality:- the state of things as they actually exist, as opposed to an idealistic or notional idea of them.

5. Possibility:- a thing that may happen or be the case.

6. Actuality:- the state of existing in reality.

7. Positivity:- the practice of being or tendency to be positive or optimistic in attitude.

8. Clarity:- the quality of transparency or purity.

9. Diversity:- the state of being diverse; variety.

10. Vanity:- excessive pride in or admiration of one's own appearance or achievements.

11. Diety:- a god or goddess.

12. Cecity:- blindness.

6. Keep Your Try On!!!

When this not your real and actual zonation,
Why bother and criticize the very creation;
Long way ahead so do bear the suffocation:
With lots of patience show your capacitation.

Convince your mind with firm intimation,
Life is an impermanent circus so action and action;
May be you might not soon attain the very perfection:
Still move on to achieve the real ambition.

You keep on working focalise wait not for attention,
When your excellence is on there
is no rooms for confusion;
Apply your mind and give your contribution:
To our nation, our universe which
has given you protection.

When you are strong and brave with godly conviction,
What wrong can happen, as you are
a mastery in dedication;
Once or twice we may fail with utter dejection:
But still keep on trying with firm determination.
**We will dare not accept defeat but shall
pulverize distraction.**

Meaning:-

1. *Zonation:- distribution in zones or regions of definite character.*

2. *Creation:- the action or process of bringing something into existence.*

3. *Suffocation:- the state or process of dying from being deprived of air or unable to breathe.*

4. *Capacitation:- to make capable; enable*

5. *Intimation:- the action of making something known, especially in an indirect way.*

6. *Action:- the fact or process of doing something, typically to achieve an aim.*

7. *Perfection:- the state or quality of being perfect.*

8. *Ambition:- a strong desire to do or achieve something.*

9. *Attention:- the action of dealing with or taking special care of someone or something.*

10. *Confusion:- uncertainty about what is happening, intended, or required.*

11. *Contribution:- a gift or payment to a common fund or collection.*

12. *Protectiion:- the action of protecting, or the state of being protected.*

13. *Conviction:- a firmly held belief or opinion.*

14. *Dedication:- the quality of being dedicated or committed to a task or purpose.*

15. *Determination:- the quality of being determined; firmness of purpose.*

16. *Distraction:- extreme agitation of the mind.*

7. My Mother Nature

Roaring strongly is my true spiritual lionize,

She is a mesmerizing author & a super poetize;

Without any reminder into height she could rise,

She spreads love in abundance & no one she criticize;

She a super affectionate mighty mother is all I realize!!!

She was high-lighting passion in every action
is for sure I apprize,

Mute by nature, joyful in her every stature, who else she is
my mother nature is all I realise!!!

Meaning:-

1. Apprize:- value highly; esteem.

2. Poetize:- write or speak in verse or in a poetic style.

3. Lionize:- female lion.

8. Soothing Echo

Oh my dear you be known for nobility-

Don't suffer totally in imbecility,

Highlight your pragmaticality-

Outwit these wisest in reality;

Realize soon your capability,

Nothing ends up in nullity-

Let your writings be full of quality;

Your every sentence emphasize logicality,

Say good bye to laziness & move in agility-

And life is all inclusive so live in compatibility:

Be steady; be steadfast to your fullest ability,

Let your entire presence in life be full of utility;

Never tolerate & accept that you are a disability-

Let all the people praise your acts and say what a personality!

Never suffer in haziness rather fine
tune & bring in super clarity.

Meaning:-

1. *Nobility:- the quality of being noble in character, goodness.*

2. *Imbecility:- of being extremely stupid.*

3. *Pragmaticality:- in a sensible and realistic way that is based on practical rather than theoretical considerations.*

4. *Reality:- the state of things as they actually exist, as opposed to an idealistic or notional idea of them.*

5. Capability:- the power or ability to do something.

6. Nullity:- the state of being null.

7. Quality:- the standard of something as measured against other things of a similar kind; the degree of excellence of something.

8. Logicality:- correct and valid reasoning

9. Agility:- ability to move quickly and easily.

10. Compatibility:- a state in which two things are able to exist or occur together without problems or conflict.

11. Ability:- possession of the means or skill to do something.

12. Utility:- the state of being useful, profitable, or beneficial.

13. Disability:- a physical or mental condition that limits a person's movements, senses, or activities.

9. Lessons for Life

Hey you never ever be impatient and infuriate,

Be so very careful to balance among love & hate;

Short is life's journey so make it sweet my affectionate,

And when failure defeat's you, don't blame on fate;

Be your own yardstick of comparison oh my great,

All the unwanted mucky of mind you abate-

All your ego, laziness & negations you devastate;

For all innovative ideas you open up mind's gate,

Super practical thoughts you do share & state;

Why shout ferociously screech in bate?

Don't contaminate yourself rather hied towards kate.

Meaning:-

1. Infuriate:- make (someone) extremely angry and impatient.

2. Abate:- to become less strong and intense.

3. Devastate:- to destroy or ruin.

4. Bate:- an angry mood.

5. Kate:-Purity.

10. Inspiring Lessons

When hurdles hit you, boom, don't be furious;

No matter what let your efforts be continuous;

Let come what may, face life oh my outrageous;

Learn, lead & love be your mantra oh my ostentatious,

Short & sweet is life's journey which at times is mysterious,

Devastate from your dictionary
the laziness which is infectious,

For a single problem give variety of solutions
in the mode of zealous;

When you are born for a noble cause focalize not be anxious!

All the honest efforts surely are meritorious;

Oh the capable youth don't become imperious,

Such you contribute holistically oh my ambitious-

Even before difficulties hit you, you be cautious,

Such you master & achieve oh my pretentious;

But for speeches & debates you be super contentious.

Meaning:-

1. *Outrageous:- very bold and courageous.*

2. *Infectious:- producing or capable of producing infection*

3. *Continuous:- marked by uninterrupted extension in space, time, or sequence.*

4. *Mysterious:- something not understood or beyond understanding.*

5.   *Zealous:- showing great energy or enthusiasm in pursuit of a cause or objective.*

6.   *Ostentatious:- characterized by pretentious or showy display; designed to impress.*

7.   *Rigorous:- extremely thorough and careful.*

8.   *Imperious:- arrogant and domineering.*

9.   *Meritorious:- deserving reward or praise.*

10. *Ambitious:- having or showing a strong desire and determination to succeed.*

11. *Furious:- full of anger or energy; violent or intense.*

12. *Cautious:- careful to avoid potential problems or dangers.*

13. *Pretentious:- (of a person) careful to avoid potential problems or dangers.*

14. *Anxious:- feeling or showing worry, nervousness, or unease about something with an uncertain outcome.*

15. *Contentious:- causing or likely to cause an argument; controversial.*

11. Simply Motivate

Never in hyper mode one should enthuse?

And illogically in folly no one you abuse?

When crime calls don't accept but seriously refuse!

You stay in a balanced mindset you don't effuse!!!

Be a large hearted one & mistakes you excuse,

From within all the motivation you produce;

And when it comes to study you just peruse,

All the learnt morals & affirmations you just diffuse;

When life throws hurdles at you
why do you end up in confuse?

Socialize & mingle with people why end up in recluse?

Meaning:-

1. *Enthuse:- express eager enjoyment, interest, or approval regarding something.*

2. *Abuse:- to use something in a bad or dishonest way.*

3. *Refuse:- to say or show that you do not want to do, give, or accept something.*

4. *Effuse:- talk in an unrestrained, excited manner.*

5. *Excuse:- a reason (that may or may not be true) that you give in order to explain your behaviour.*

6. *Produce:- manufacture, to make something to be sold, especially in large quantities.*

7. *Peruse:- to read something, especially in a careful way.*

8. *Diffuse:- to spread something or become spread widely in all directions.*

9. *Confuse:- to make somebody unable to think clearly or to know what to do.*

10. *Recluse:- a religious person who lives a life away from other people and society.*

12. Hearty Message

Stay triumphantly joyful & stay blissful,

With all the hopes on be far-sightful;

For this entire planet you be useful-

Do your every do by being cheerful,

Say not I am tired & be restful:

Let there be no rooms for sadness, sorrow & doleful!

Meaning:-

1. *Blissful:- extremely happy; full of joy.*

2. *Farsightful:- having good judgment about what will be needed in the future and making wise decisions.*

3. *Doleful:- expressing sorrow; mournful.*

13. To my Enlightened Master!

For sure I will spread all your teachings far & wide-

I am engrossed in learning from morning to eventide,

I am an open book of yours so what else shall I hide?

Then why you think & worry keep your tensions aside;

Each & every second I am enjoying this life's joyful ride-

You are a diety of knowledge & wisdom I say with pride,

Well, I will surely fulfill all your needs for always in fide;

All morals & virtues of yours I am here to simply abide;

I will promote your messages & affirmations worldwide,

**Oh the guru you are beside or
aside & everywhere you reside.**

Meaning:-

1. Eventide:- the end of the day; evening

2. Aside:- to one side; out of the way.

3. Ride:- sit on and control the movement of (an animal, typically a horse).

4. Fide:- neither specious nor counterfeit : genuine.

5. Abide:- accept or act in accordance with (a rule, decision, or recommendation).

6. Reside:- have one's permanent home in a particular place.

14. Oh the Monkey Mind

Don't carry filth in your mucky mind!
Purity from within you always find,
All the positives you just selfishly bind;
Stay blest and happy oh the super mind-
But for intellect you be that mastermind,
You are born to achieve oh the wunderkind;
Be generous have sympathy to be that humankind,
Past worries & future anxieties you don't rewind & unwind;
Bring in the lost smile on every face
oh the dear super mind.

Meaning:-
1. *Filth:- Dirt*
2. *Mucky:- Dirt*

15. Just Do This

Develop some strong love for mother nation;

Be an inspiring soul of super high aspiration;

Be known for innate focus & concentration;

Joyful you be everyday with happy emotion,

Be known for your teachings & affirmation-

Sell your wit & talent is my steadfast caution;

Life is a huge co-ordinated symphony of action,

Let there be no deficiency for love and affection,

Let there be no rooms for commotion & distraction;

Be open for risks and don't end up in circumspection;

But for all positive traits you hie towards acquisition-

You be your own yardstick of comparison & competition;

Have a balanced mindset & don't end up in galvanization,

**Knowing that you are a speck
in this cosmos be the realization;**

**Keeping the focus and skill very tight
is all be the prioritization.**

Meaning:-

1. *Nation:- Country*

2. *Aspiration:-A hope or ambition to achieve something*

3. *Concentration:- The action a power of focusing all one's action*

4. Emotion:- A strong feeling deriving from one's circumstances mood or relationships with others.

5. Affirmation:- Emotional support or encouragement.

6. Caution:- care taken to danger and mistakes

7. Action:- the fact or process of doing somethingtypically to achieve an aim.

8. Affection:- A gentle feeling of fondless or liking.

9. Distraction:- A thing that prevents someone from concentration of something.

10. Circumspection:- the quality of being wary & unwilling to take risks, prudence.

11. Acquisition:- the learning or developing of a skill, habit or quality.

12. Competition:- rivalry

13. Galvanization:- shock or excited in taking action.

14. Realisation:- an act of becoming fully aware of something as a fact.

15. Prioritisation:- the action or process of deciding the relative importance or urgency of a thing or things.

16. My True Wish!

Why in folly dissolve in the pool of entanglement?

When failure arrives don't end up in disappointment,

Spread your joyful smile to everyone in every moment;

Never get disturbed when foes give a negative comment;

When I am always there to protect
you why end up in lament,

When you excel well at work it naturally
leads to accomplishment;

Be very wise & astute when it comes
to taking a right judgement,

Let all your inspiration increase with all the encouragement,

When time is precious why waste time in illogical argument;

When you are defeated in life don't end up in resentment,

In every work you do, do it in the mode of vehement;

Strongly fight against and root out unemployment,

Leak creative ideas is my strong announcement;

Stay far far away from bewilderment.

Meaning:-

1. Entanglement:- cause to become twisted together with or caught in.

2. Disappointment:- sadness or displeasure caused by the non-fulfilment of one's hopes or expectations.

3. Moment:- a very brief period of time.

4. Comment:- a verbal or written remark expressing an opinion or reaction.

5. Lament:- a passionate expression of grief or sorrow.

6. Accomplishment:- something that has been achieved successfully.

7. Judgement:- the ability to make considered decisions or come to sensible conclusions.

8. Encouragement:- the action of giving someone support, confidence, or hope.

9. Argument:- a reason or set of reasons given in support of an idea, action or theory

10. Resentment:- bitter indignation at having been treated unfairly.

11. Vehement:- showing strong feeling; forceful, passionate, or intense.

12. Unemployment:- the state of being unemployed.

13. Announcement:- a formal public statement about a fact, occurrence, or intention.

14. Bewilderment:- a feeling of being perplexed and confused.

17. Seek this Only Mantra

You be known for victory, oh the mastermind,

Don't ignore the distorted experience of mind,

Say not I am fragile even when you are behind;

All the past & future anxieties you do not rewind,

Serve, lead, inspiringly educate the entire mankind,

You are just born only to achieve oh the supermind-

For all the hard questions super solutions you outfind;

In motivational mode teach the entire world & remind,

**That with a burning desire to achieve
you be that humankind.**

Meaning:-

1. *Mastermind:- a person with an outstanding intellect.*

2. *Mind:- the element of a person that enables them to be aware of the world and their experiences, to think, and to feel; the faculty of consciousness and thought.*

3. *Behind:- at the back of.*

4. *Rewind:- to make a recording go back towards the beginning:*

5. *Mankind:- the whole of the human race, including both men and women.*

6. *Supermind:- a mind, or a thing that is like a mind, that is more powerful than an ordinary mind, especially when it is created by a large number of people or computers working together*

7. *Remind:- cause (someone) to remember someone or something.*

8. *Humankind:- human beings considered collectively (used as a neutral alternative to 'mankind').*

18. Ideas to Implement

Just bowing down to your almighty is all the notion,

Be on your heels to achieve your goal in perk action;

Tremendously love, respect & worship mother nation,

Being meditative even in this entire universal mansion,

Ignite the light of the mind's deep intuitive dimension,

Increasing your wit is the only smart & fabulous option;

You in your entire life give rooms for creative imagination;

Make your body a consecrated place is my steadfast caution;

Oh the solution giving human give answers to every question,

Keep your joyful face on of happy emotion;

Learn all the morals & virtues by adaptation,

Remembering god, you ecstatically dance in elation,

So strongly and simply admire the creator & creation;

Oh the dear human be known & hied towards donation,

From your body all the positives just come out in eruption;

And work so productively that you soon
reach highest position.

Meaning:-

1. *Notion:- a conception of or belief about something.*

2. *Action:- the fact or process of doing something, typically to achieve an aim.*

3. *Nation:- country.*

4. *Mansion:-home.*

5. *Dimention:- a measurable extent of a particular kind, such as length, breadth, depth, or height.*

6. *Option:- a thing that is or may be chosen.*

7. *Imagination:- the faculty or action of forming new ideas, or images or concepts of external objects not present to the senses.*

8. *Caution:- care taken to avoid danger or mistakes.*

9. *Question:- querry*

10. *Emotion:- a strong feeling deriving from one's circumstances, mood, or relationships with others.*

11. *Adaptation:- the action or process of adapting or being adapted.*

12. *Elation:- great happiness and exhilaration.*

13. *Creation:- the action or process of bringing something into existence.*

14. *Donation:- something that is given to a charity, especially a sum of money.*

15. *Position:- a place where someone or something is located or has been put.*

16. *Eruption:- an act or instance of erupting.*

19. Teach

Why boldly lie confidently,

Go against the inner conscious abruptly;

Milestones you achieve quietly,

Be practical & think logically;

Let your soothing touch be gently,

Stronger you grow rightly;

Ignite the light in all brightly,

Spread smile on every face vastly;

Educate everyone too subtly,

Lead a sense-ful life joyfully;

Hey you strongly grow boldly,

When people hurt you don't cry sadly;

And dissolve in the pool of negations madly,

Believe in your strengths widely;

Help the poor & needy kindly.

Meaning:-

1. *Confidently:- in a self-assured way that expresses faith in oneself or one's abilities or qualities.*

2. *Abruptly:- suddenly and unexpectedly.*

3. *Quietly:- in a quiet manner.*

4. *Logically:- according to the rules of logic or formal argument.*

5. Gently:- with a mild, kind, or tender manner.

6. Rightly:- correctly.

7. Brightly:- in a way that gives out or reflects much light, in an intelligent and quick-witted way.

8. Vastly:- to a very great extent; immensely.

9. Subtly:- in a manner that is so delicate or precise as to be difficult to analyse or describe, in a high level.

10. Joyfully:- with great pleasure and happiness.

11. Boldly:- in a confident and courageous way; showing a willingness to take risks.

12. Sadly:- in agony

13. Madly:- in a mad, wild, or uncontrolled manner

14. Widely:- far apart.

15. Kindly:- in a kind manner.

20. A Lyrical Echo

Don't react in hyper mode and galvanize,

Be in a balanced mind set oh poetize!

Be cool be calm to just realise,

That there is a lot to learn so prioritize.

Let nothing be visible except your emprise,

Here and there are too many hurdles and obelize,

When else will you exercise your patience you just utilise;

On a regular basis you just focalise.

Exercise your efforts, don't just idolize,

Radiate courage and strength my lionize;

Spread positive vibes rather don't elegize!

Make new mistakes and at the end you specialise!

Meaning:-

1. galvanize- Shock or excite (someone) into taking action.

2. Obelize- Mark (a word or passage) with an obelus to show that it is spurious, corrupt, or doubtful.

3. Emprise- A purpose, an intention.

4. Lionize- Give a lot of public attention and approval to (someone); treat as a celebrity.

5. Idiolize- Admire, revere, or love greatly or excessively.

6. Elegize- write in a wistfully mournful way.

21. Time to Learn

When you become a nation builder and a world architect!

You are born to inspire & spread love & joy to every object,

The power of your inborn possibility into every life you inject;

But from all possible relationships you just don't really expect!

All the negations & false believes you
simply simply just deject,

Why after-all you hopelessly drastically fail you don't abject;

Such you strongly grow! that negations wont affect!

As you are born to outgrow every hurdle and defect;

Such you purify oneself that there is no place for infect,

Oh the candid perky human be joyful in life's every aspect!

Be an entire museum of positivity so the same you just reflect,

Nip the very feeling of laziness & sleep
the moment you detect!

You are born to love, learn & lead in the mode of perfect;

Be all inclusive in life! Love every life every insect;

From your entire body haziness you eject!

When it comes to politics the capable one you elect!

Meaning:-

1. Architect:- a person who is qualified to design buildings and to plan and supervise their construction.

2. Object:- thing

3.   Inject:- to insert

4.   Expect:- regard (something) as likely to happen.

5.   Deject:- make sad or dispirited; depress.

6.   Abject:- (of a person or their behaviour) completely without pride or dignity; self-abasing.

7.   Reflect:- (of a surface or body) throw back (heat, light, or sound) without absorbing it.

8.   Detect:- discover or identify the presence or existence of.

9.   Direct:- aim (something) in a particular direction or at a particular person

10. Insect:- a type of small animal with six legs, a body divided into three parts, and often two pairs of wings, for example, an ant, beetle, or butterfly

11. Eject:- to push, throw, or force something out of a place

12. Elect:- to decide on or choose.

22. Innovative Mother

She was soaring high into lofty heights of creativity,

What super great lexicon power she processed in reality;

Innovative & visionary ideas she
was spreading, look at her capability!

In her each & every stride she was highlighting unlimited
exuberant possibility,

During people's all possible difficult times she
was their strong credibility;

This brilliantly philliantrophic mother was rendering her helping
hand to everyone in actuality,

This intense meditative lady was leaking stupendous
insights obliterating vanity!

In her each & every act she was
promoting love, care and purity,

Who else she is universal mother endorsing parity;

In her entire presence there is no discrimination, jealousy,
perk in abundance, ruling entire cosmos as her own polity
and thus entire life seems a super perky possibility!!!

Meaning:-

1. *Vanity:- the quality of being worthless or futile.*

2. *Verity:- A primary true principle or belief.*

3. *Credibility:- the quality trusted and believed in.*

4. *Polity:- A political organization.*

5. *Parity:- Equality.*

23. Strong Message

She is a courageous lady of noble character,
A cheerful clearheaded lady who is my protective partner;
Hillarious & ebbulient innovative & souciant,
My eternal encyclopedia & a huge spiritually riant-
Brilliantly smart, extraordinarily farsighted;
For innumerable people bliss she has initiated,
Felicific & aesthetically, dynamic & earnest,
Independent & perky, genuinely gentle & decent;
Forthrightly generous, hearty & heroic,
blemishless in appearance, orderly & patriotic;
Liberal & mature an optimist who is organized,
Passionate at work with a blend of perk is all I have realised;
Profound & protective, prudent & rational,
Highly responsible of reverential insight & sensational;
Sane, scholarly, scrupulous and secure,
Truly religious whose heart is immensely pure-
Self defacing, self made, self reliant & self sufficient;
Extreamly brilliant and super efficient-
Relaxed & reliable, resourseful & respectful,
Stably, steadfast, simple & brilliantly joyful!
Strong & reliable, sweet & sympathetic,
Tidy &, tactful & trustful & empathetic;

Understanding & trustful vivaciously wise,

All her traits people stand in queue to praise-

Charismatic & creative of determined insight;

Who else she is my gleaming mother bright-

Diligent and easy going, cooperative and clever,

Is my sweet holy mother who by choice a super giver!!!

Meaning:-

1. *Character:- the mental and moral qualities distinctive to an individual.*

2. *Partner:- either of a pair of people engaged together in the same activity.*

3. *Souciant:- to be conerned about, to worry about, to care about.*

4. *Riant:- laughing; smiling; cheerful*

5. *Farsighted:- unable to see things clearly, especially if they are relatively close to the eyes; long-sighted.*

6. *Initiated:- a person who has been initiated into an organization or activity.*

7. *Earnest:- resulting from or showing sincere and intense conviction.*

8. *Decent:- conforming with generally accepted standards of respectable or moral behaviour.*

9. *Heroic:- having the characteristics of a hero or heroine; admirably brave or determined.*

10. *Patriotic:- having or expressing devotion to and vigorous support for one›s country.*

11. *Organized:- Well Ordered*

12. *Realised:-* become fully aware of (something) as a fact; understand clearly.

13. *Rational:-* based on or in accordance with reason or logic.

14. *Sensational:-* causing great public interest and excitement.

15. *Secure:-* certain to remain safe and unthreatened.

16. *Pure:-* not mixed or adulterated with any other substance or material.

17. *Self sufficient:-* needing no outside help in satisfying one's basic needs, especially with regard to the production of food.

18. *Efficient:-* (of a person) working in a well-organized and competent way.

19. *Respectful:-* feeling or showing deference and respect.

20. *Joyful:-* feeling, expressing, or causing great pleasure and happiness.

21. *Sympathetic:-* Pitying

22. *Empathetic:-* showing an ability to understand and share the feelings of another.

23. *Wise:-* having or showing experience, knowledge, and good judgement.

24. *Praise:-* express warm approval or admiration of.

25. *Insight:-* the capacity to gain an accurate and deep understanding of someone or something.

26. *Bright:-* giving out or reflecting much light; shining.

27. *Clever:-* quick to understand, learn, and devise or apply ideas; intelligent.

28. *Giver:-* a person who gives something.

24. Motivational Words

Let all get mesmerized by you being devout,

Intensely perky be your life is all about;

Sleep and intense anger you just clean out,

From the world of laziness you just logout;

But for all negations you just simply box out,

And for lethargy you just nip it before it pops out-

Always in fear, agony & sadness a Why hopelessly shout;

During failure don't lose faith & trust & dont back out-

Be known for inspiration in all your life be throughout,

Let joyful relationships you just strongly build out;

Lots to teach & learn be your mantra so chill out;

**Let the possibility of your positivity lead
to enlightenment so joyfully check out.**

Meaning:-

1. *Devout:- having or showing deep religious feeling or commitment.*

2. *About:- on the subject of; concerning.*

3. *Clean out:- on the subject of concerning.*

4. *Log out:- an act of logging out of a computer system.*

5. *Boxout:- a piece of text written to accompany a larger text and printed in a separate area of the page.*

6. *Pops out*

25. Flirting with Deathly God !!!

Oh dreadly death ! oh dreadly death !
You seem to attack on all you see:
Oh dreadly death ! oh dreadly death !
You are too early is what I wholly see.

Oh dreadly death ! oh dreadly death !
Uff. . . your adamancy and urgency;
Oh dreadly death ! oh dreadly death !
Still life is on don't you see?

Oh dreadly death ! oh dreadly death !
Look lives are building dreams on dreams;
Oh dreadly death ! oh dreadly death !
Don't shatter their heart dreamt dreams.

Oh dreadly death ! oh dreadly death !
My words have made you frown:-
Oh dreadly death ! oh dreadly death !
Still there so much to know and learn.

Oh dreadly death ! oh dreadly death !
I am neither boasting for the renown,
Oh dreadly death ! oh dreadly death !
Your presence itself is for sure then:
Let me see, let me fight alone,
Let me fight alone!!!

26. Thoughtful Message

Why suffer in the mode of destitute?

Rather stay in a balanced mindset of astute,

But for achievements you universally contribute;

Stay high upon the success ladder oh the captain absolute!

When success comes show the gratitude of high tribute!

Just with immense joy & perk every job you execute,

To that great almighty why don't you salute?

Stay flexible in life like the angle acute.

Meaning:-

1. Destitute: extremely poor and lacking the means to provide for oneself.

2. Astute: sharp-witted.

27. Mother of Tolerance my Mother Universe!!!

Long long ago from time immemorial,

There lived a selfless self-made lady on hills,

A truly devoted diehard fan of the godhead,

Who was just here to sing, exercise, study, jot, dance and meditate.

Actually, everyone all were dumbstruck then,

"How will she ever lead a life like this then?".

Her patience her goodness was but in abundance,

There was no comparison for her tunes of melody,

Her love for nature, her love for animals,

She inwardly outwardly a very strong person,

She an inspiring lady, a lady of solutions.

While watering the plants,

While cooking the food,

While drafting inspiring poems,

While planting the saplings,

While making the pots,

While singing the ballads,

While walking down the lane,

She was but engrossed in her lord's memories.

At times forgetting herself completely on the whole,

Immersed in the chant of the very divine,

"Was she the real mother who had jumped from heaven???"

As she saw god in each and every person,

All loved her, all adored her,

She was a super leader everywhere she stepped,

She eradicated hurdles and brought in perky joy,

She, a guiding gaurd for us but a super perfect devotee, fan of her own master.

She a colourful personality kid's all-time favourite,

Though she seemed very simple out,

But was complicated from within,

Her mastery in the art of perfection,

Reflects in her each and every action,

What not she knew, she knew herself completely,

She was here just to meditate, lead and teach us all,

As her boundless affection had no fullstop.

Mother I can feel you, mother I can see all your holistic actions you are but a blessing in disguise oh mother you are but a blessing in disguise!!!

28. Inspiring Thought

Why groan and cry with an unhappy feel,

And complain & howl that nothing can heal;

Conquer entire universe with your motivational appeal,

Learn, lead & love be the mantra but procastination you seal;

With the entire negation department you sign a friendly deal,

There by listning to you everytime is all the deal;

All your laziness and sleep you joyfully repeal,

Stay happy with your equanimity
on and inspiringly all you anneal.

Meaning:-

1. *Repeal:- revoke, abrogate.*

2. *Anneal:- to toughen or strengthen (the will, determination, etc)*

3. *Feel:- If you feel a particular emotion or physical sensation, you experience it.*

4. *Heal:- cause (a wound, injury, or person) to become sound or healthy again.*

5. *Appeal:- make a serious, urgent, or heartfelt request.*

6. *Seal:- fasten or close securely.*

7. *Deal:- an agreement entered into by two or more parties for their mutual benefit, especially in a business or political context.*

29. Mother Almighty

She is bursting out in the mode of giety,

She was highlighting enormous responsibility;

She was screeching "soon know your capability,

But for comparision you be your own yardstick in reality;

Don't just let your mind get distracted so pity,

In your every activity highlight the clarity;

Staying strong be your own true ability,

Even among intoxicated pollution you spread purity;

Then there by confidence and will power you leak in plenty,

So who else she is that is all she says my mother mighty."

Meaning:-

1. Gaiety:- happy.

2. Responsibility:- the state or fact of having a duty to deal with something or of having control over someone.

3. Capability:- the power or ability to do something.

4. Reality:- real life.

5. Pity:- Compassion.

6. Ability:- possession of the means or skill to do something.

7. Purity:- freedom from adulteration or contamination.

8. Plenty:- vast

9. Mighty:- strong.

10. Clarity:- the quality of being coherent & intelligible.

30. When Learn is On!!!

Arise with potent not in dullness;

Leave all your dimness & badness,

Be filled with joy & holistic richness,

Speak to people in the mode of kindness,

Suffer not in shameness not even in sadness,

Leave all the smallness and grow in bigness;

Be a huge ocean of sweet intimacy & oneness!

When it comes to body be known for fitness;

Respect your almighty that is your highness;

Think in the mode of broadmindedness,

Give not space for blindness & darkness;

In every sentence enjoy smartly the art of new wordiness;

Become a huge encyclopedia in happiness,

Glow strongly in vividness and perkiness;

Short is life's journey make it sweet my nobleness,

Oh the eloquent fiery youth be full of aliveness.

Eradicate timidness stay brave without proudness;

Oh the courageous youth you enjoy aloneness,

Ignite the light in all & suffer not in twilightness,

Why be a taker always you give in delightness;

Be the giver of knowledge & wisdom in cheerfulness,

With felicity & exuberance you empower all in blissfulness,

**Be known a dictionary oh the modish
youth suffer not in nerdiness!!!**

Meaning:-

1. *Dullness:- paleness*
2. *Badness:- not good*
3. *Richness:- the quality of being kind*
4. *Kindness:- the quality of being kind*
5. *Sadness:- the feeling of being unhappy*
6. *Bigness:- of large in size*
7. *Oneness:- the fact or state of being unified & being one in number*
8. *Fitness:- The condition of being physically fit and healthy*
9. *Highness:- a tittle given of a person of royal rank*
10. *Broadmindedness:- willing to accept many different types of behavior belief and choices.*
11. *Darkness:- Absence of light*
12. *Blissfullness:- extreamely happy and joy*
13. *Happiness:- state of being happy.*
14. *Perkiness:- the quality or state of being happy and full of energy*
15. *Nobleness:- the quality of elevation of mind & character*
16. *Aliveness :- living, not dead*
17. *Proudness:- having or showing respect for oneself*
18. *Aloneness:- solitude*
19. *Twilightness:- the period or state of ambiguity*
20. *Delightness:- great pleasure*
21. *Cheerfullness:- the quality or state of being happy and optimistic*
22. *Wordiness:- the quality of containing too many words*

31. Inspiring Message

Don't whimper sadly in agony,

When hurdles arrive you be stony;

Learn to live joyfully in harmony,

Don't say that you are worthlessly loony;

You playfully romance the entire universe
platonically in the mode of moony.

Meaning:-

1. *Agony:- extreme physical or mental suffering.*

2. *Loony:- A mad or silly person.*

3. *Moony:- dreamy and unaware of one's surroundings, for example because one is in love.*

4. *Stony:- not having feelings or showing feeling not of sympathy.*

32. Simple Learn

You be known for spotlessness,

Sell your wit not your foolishness;

And everywhere promote your shabbiness,

Nothing wrong in making flaws & blemishness;

Why be hopelessly conscious of your unworthiness?

Be that dynamo which leaks steadiness,

Do your every do with aptness;

Why blindly live life in opaqueness?

You're born to be joyful do not stay in dullness,

Let your transperancy speak in astuteness,

You are born to live in aliveness;

Just let your equanimity speak in sereness.

Meaning:-

1. Spotlessness:- the state of being spotlessly clean.

2. Shabbiness:- he quality of looking old or in bad condition because of being used for a long time or not being cared for.

3. Blemishes:- a small mark or flaw which spoils the appearance of something.

4. Unworthiness:- of lacking merit or value worthiness

5. Steadiness:- the quality not shaking or moving.

6. Aptness:- the quality of being appropriate or suitable.

7. Opaqueness:- the characteristic of being either difficult to see through or hard to understand.

8. *Dullness:- lack of interest or excitement.*

9. *Astuteness:- the quality of being able to quickly understand a situation and see how to get an advantage from it*

10. *Aliveness:- full of exuberance*

11. *Foolishness:- mufffness*

12. *Sereness:- a state of freedom from storm or disturbance.*

33. Advice

Nobody is Mr. Wrong nobody is Mr. Right,

Then why in folly you do fight?

To just focus you go there straight,

During the journey you don't fright;

Eradicate darkness by your light,

Stay strong with all the might;

By then regret not in plight,

Glow and gleam my dear bright;

In this life's journey be full of delight,

Oh the mastermind you are born to achieve alright?

In your action, passion and determination you highlight,

Such you master meditation of full-fledged foresight;

Seeing things as it is be your eyesight;

Ego, ignorance & laziness you do fight,

Why end up foolishly in catfight?

Strongly outshine even in twilight!!

Meaning:-

1. *Fight:-* Quarrel

2. *Straight:-* extending or moving uniformly in one direction only; without a curve or bend.

3. *Light:-* the natural agent that stimulates sight and makes things visible. Illumination

4.   Might:- Strength

5.   Plight:- a dangerous, difficult, or otherwise unfortunate situation.

6.   Fright:- a sudden intense feeling of fear.

7.   Advice:- Guidance

8.   Bright:- gleaming strongly

9.   Delight:- happiness

10.   Alright:- Saying okay, agree

11.   Highlight:- draw special attention to.

12.   Faresight:- having or showing foresight or good judgment, sagacious.

13.   Eyesight:- a person's ability to see.

14.   Catfight:- a fight between women.

15.   Twilight:-Darkness

16.   Right:- morally good, justified, or acceptable

17.   Advice:- a suggestion about what someone should do.

34. Inspirational Solution

You all know that life isn't all our planned itenary,

Still you realize that you aren't an ordinary;

You are born to outgrow the extraordinary,

By then suffer not in the mode of solitary;

Bravely fight out all your enemies & adversary,

Oh the noble one, you outwit the visionary;

Such you master people call you a dictionary,

Creative of the creative ideas you give of imaginary;

Realise that these momentary pleasures are but temporary,

Such you live people must call u a gift of complementary;

Let the sole aim be visible rest all are secondary,

Among all let the focus be the primary.

Meaning:-

1. *Itenary:- a plan of a journey, including the route and the places that you will visit.*

2. *Ordinary:- with no special or distinctive features; normal.*

3. *Extroardinary:- very unusual or remarkable.*

4. *Solitary:- Lonely*

5. *Adversary:- one that contends with, opposes, or resists: an enemy or opponent.*

6. *Visionary:- thinking about or planning the future with imagination or wisdom.*

7. Dictionary:- a reference book listing alphabetically terms or names important to a particular subject or activity along with discussion of their meanings and applications

8. Imaginary:- lacking factual reality

9. Temporary:- one serving for a limited time

10. Complementary:- related to each other in such a way that one completes the other.

11. Secondary:- coming after, less important than, or resulting from someone or something else that is primary.

12. Primary:- of chief importance; principal.

35. A Short Ode

I will strive, work & sweat for a great vision,

Yes I am just born to lead all with a firm mission;

Empowering every citizen to build a strong nation,

Not just this nation but entire universe is my mansion

Let your every do highlight high commitment & passion;

Working smart to inspire all be your steadfast realisation,

Let in mind let there be no time
for the very confusion & delusion.

Meaning:-

1. *Vision:- the faculty or state of being able to see.*

2. *Mission:- an important job, especially a military one, that someone is sent somewhere to do*

3. *Nation:- country*

4. *Mansion:- house, home*

5. *Passion:- an extreme interest in or wish for doing something, such as a hobby, activity, etc.:*

6. *Realisation:- the state of being aware of or understanding a situation deeply n being thoughtful*

7. *Confusion:- ambiguity*

8. *Delusion:- a false belief or judgment about external reality*

36. Seek the Lesson

Shower loads of love on this creation;

You go bond with the ties of affection,

Strongly worship Bharat, mother nation,

Let us joyfully sing the song of toleration;

Think whole universe as our actual zonation,

You be patient, you persevere is all the notion;

Inject & spread in all perky energy by elocution,

Spreading "LOVE," the universal language
of your master be the paction.

Meaning:-

1. *Affection:- : a feeling of liking and caring for someone or something : tender attachment : FONDNESS*

2. *Creation:- the action or process of bringing something into existence.*

3. *Nation:- a large body of people united by common descent, history, culture, or language, inhabiting a particular country or territory.*

4. *Toleration:- Toleration is the practice of allowing or putting up with something, especially if you disagree with it.*

5. *Zonation:- distribution in zones or regions of definite character.*

6. *Notion:- a conception of or belief about something*

7. *Elocution:- the skill of clear and expressive speech, especially of distinct pronunciation and articulation*

8. *Paction:-agreement, compact, bargain.*

37. Simple Message

Highlight clarity in your action not stupefy;

Oh my darling your playful life is there to gamify,

Train your mind such that you introspect & modify,

Thatz how legends are made you can surely verify;

Since god lives in your heart so you just glorify,

You're born to learn, lead & love so I notify,

Quell all the hatred, agitation & do pacify;

Enjoy your every do & vivify;

But for smartness & brilliance you exemplify.

Meaning:-

1. *Gamify:-* To make an activity more like a game in order to make it more interesting & enjoyable.

2. *Stupefy:-* make someone unable to think or feel properly.

3. *Glorify:-* Praise & worship.

4. *Agitation:-* Worry & anxiety.

5. *Pacify:-* Maintain calmness.

6. *Notify:-* Inform someone of something.

7. *Vivify:-* Make more lively & interesting, enliven.

8. *Exemplify:-* Be an epitome of.

38. Lessons of Motivation

Why suffer in unbridled flights of fancy,

Rather be a super huge logical agency;

Lead the people through your captaincy,

Move on in life without regret & hesitancy;

Dear be known for decency & brilliancy,

When hurdles defeat, you react in resilency;

Enjoy life in joy & perk with bouncy,

Realise the power of possibility & efficiency;

Oh the ruler of mind be known for flamboyancy,

Obliterate from your dictionary the word inconsistency;

Experience the unlimited joy through regularity & constancy,

Be that unshakable power of truth of high vibrancy;

Be that selfmade human being without dependency;

Be the giver of solutions by self-sufficiency,

Why time & again suffer in insufficiency,

Let your every do be full of competency;

Increase purity of mind through sheer transparency.

Meaning:-

1. *Fancy:- elaborate in structure or decoration.*

2. *Agency:- a business or organization providing a particular service on behalf of another business, person, or group.*

3. Captaincy:- the position or period of command over a team, ship, or aircraft.

4. Hesitancy:- lack of willingness or eagerness to do something : reluctance.

5. Brilliancy:- exceptional talent or intelligence.

6. Resistency:- the refusal to accept or comply with something.

7. Bouncy:- bouncing or causing things to bounce.

8. Efficiency:- the state or quality of being efficient, or able to accomplish something with the least waste of time and effort; competency in performance.

9. Flamboyancy:- the quality of being very confident in your behaviour, and liking to be noticed by other people, for example because of the way you dress or talk:

10. Inconsistency:- the fact or state of being inconsistent.

11. Constancy:- the quality of being faithful and dependable.

12. Vibrancy:- the state of being full of energy and life.

13. Dependency:- a country or province controlled by another.

14. Sufficiency:- the condition or quality of being adequate or sufficient.

15. Insufficiency:- the condition of being insufficient.

16. Competency:- Competency is the ability to use a set of skills for a specific work that needs critical task functions.

17. Transperancy:- the quality of being easily seen through

39. A Ray of Light!!!

A ray of light just came with a piece of advice,
was a pure sleek light that came from far outside;
filling the whole universe with its pure bright light.

What a boundless energy!!!
it possessed indeed a very strong might.

Whenever I tried to reach at its very height,
More bigger, wider and stronger it increased its size;
"Keep your firmness right, keep your firmness tight!!
It cooly kept on singing everywhere radiating delight.

In the darkest midnight even in the brightest daylight,
It never woozily moved but was just standing up straight,
Filling the whole universe with all the love and peace;
Where not is its cool breeze?? as everywhere it is!!!

With folded hands I devotingly before it I just knelt,
Come on my child, it smiled, grabing me to its side,
Oh commitment spreading light you belong to everyone:

You belong to not just for me but you are
itself everything and everyone.

40. Student of this Cosmic School

In this entire vast cosmic school

But for lies dear you just don't drool,

When entire galaxy is my cosmic school;

Of high strong equanimity I am totally cool,

Entire cosmos is my entire karmic learning pool;

Seek knowledge, seek wisdom, through smartness tool;

Oh god here some are very smart
and but some are bloody fool,

**Rule and rule yes just remember
that you are born to rule and rule.**

Meaning:-

1. *School:- an institution for educating children.*

2. *Drool:- drop saliva uncontrollably from the mouth.*

3. *Cool:- chill*

4. *Pool:- a small area of usually still water:*

5. *Tool:- a piece of equipment that you use with your hands to make or repair something:*

6. *Fool:- foolish*

7. *Rule:- to be the most important and controlling influence on someone:*

41. Nature my Mother

She is innately shrewd by nature,
Absolutely humble in spite of stature;
She loves every animal & every creature,
Balanced whether its past, present or future;
She says 'train your mind from within nurture,
Behaving decently be your gesture;
Sitting with erect spine be your posture,
Be more sharp & attentive than a vulture;
Respect our tradition, our rich heritage & culture,
Let simplicity speak by your simple vesture;
Highly famous for giving meaningful lecture,
You are born to lead so be your innate nature.

Meaning:-

1. Nature:- the living world, creation

2. Stature:- importance or reputation gained by ability or achievement.

3. Creature:- living organism

4. Future:- a period of time following the moment of speaking or writing; time regarded as still to come.

5. Nurture:- care for and protect (someone or something) while they are growing.

6. Gesture:- a movement of part of the body, especially a hand or the head, to express an idea or meaning.

7. *Posture:- the position in which someone holds their body when standing or sitting.*

8. *Vulture:- a large bird of prey with the head and neck more or less bare of feathers*

9. *Culture:- tradition*

10. *Vesture:- Clothing or dress*

11. *Lecture:- A speech*

42. Oh the Selfmade Mind!

Stop unlimited confusion & bewilderment in the mind,
Everywhere every place spreading joy, be your kind;
Though past is behind don't forget the lessons of hind,
Oh the selfmade mind I am always there to remind.

Unnecessary wrangles in others why do you find,
Even if you are on the tip of fame don't be unkind;
All the opportunities you simply strongly bind,
Oh the selfmade mind I am always there to remind.

All the your incapabilities & negations you simply unbind,
Everyday is a holiday, this notion you keep it in mind;
Balanced and benevolent you be, oh the super mind,
Oh the selfmade mind I am always there to remind.

When sleep and laziness conquer you don't say never mind,
Working perkily and joyfully be your kind,
You are born to be that mastermind;
Oh the selfmade mind I am always there to remind.

When it comes to achievement you be wunderkind,
Answers to all questions you simply outfind;

To spread all the positives you are born oh the mastermind,
Oh the selfmade mind I am always there to remind.

Find god in humanity oh the super mind,
But for all the lives you be that humankind;
Don't weakly in fragile way say I am behind,
Oh the selfmade mind I am always there to remind.

Meaning:-

1. *Mind:- a person's ability to think and reason; the intellect.*
2. *Kind:- polite*
3. *Hind:- situated at the back; posterior*
4. *Remind:- cause (someone) to remember someone or something.*
5. *Find:- to search*
6. *Unkind:- harsh*
7. *Bind:- to cover*
8. *Unbind:- to uncover*
9. *Outfind:- to find out or discover*
10. *Mastermind:- a person with an outstanding intellect.*
11. *Supermind:- a mind, or a thing that is like a mind, that is more powerful than an ordinary mind, especially when it is created by a large number of people or computers working together*
12. *Humankind:- human beings considered collectively (used as a neutral alternative to 'mankind').*
13. *Behind:- to stay back.*
14. *Remind:- cause (someone) to remember someone or something.*

43. Inspirational Wings

She was flying with the wings of inspiration
And of high enthusiasm she says action and action
And such strongly she was worshipping mother nation
And but for actually writing, creativity is the only potion

And that she says once you are
super unique be the only option

All the time she was totally out-bursting
in severe happy ovation

If not now when will you achieve in joy
she asks this in her mansion?

Her esctatic dance and songs were highly
infinite end up in tears of devotion!!!!

Meaning:-

1. *Inspiration:- the process of being mentally stimulated to do or feel something, especially to do something creative.*

2. *Action:- the fact or process of doing something, typically to achieve an aim.*

3. *Nation:- country*

4. *Potion:- a liquid with healing, magical, or poisonous properties.*

5. *Option:- only way*

6. *Ovation:- a sustained and enthusiastic show of appreciation from an audience, especially by means of applause.*

7. *Mansion:- home, house*

44. Be that Complete Soul

There is no stupidity, no obscurity, everywhere there is ability and everywhere you ignite the lamp of possibility!!!

Meaning:-

1. *Festivity:- the celebration of something in a joyful and exuberant way.*

2. *Intellectuality:- brilliancy*

3. *Ability:- capability*

4. *Possibility:- something that is possible*

5. *Collapsibility:- to collapse down*

6. *Stability:- the state of being stable.*

7. *Versatality:- ability to adapt or be adapted to many different functions or activities.*

8. *Respectability:- to honour*

9. *Creativity:- the use of imagination or original ideas to create something; inventiveness.*

10. *Publicity:- notice or attention given to someone or something by the media.*

11. *Actuality:- reality*

12. *Sincerity:- honesty*

45. Song of the Youth

Oh the divine almighty! We are all your super creation!

Cosmos is your signature & complete administration,

Day & night you teach us the lessons of toleration;

In every birth I have your promised protection,

No matter what, first comes mother nation;

As we are already steadfastly on with firm ambition,

By burning the midnight oil we strive
to build a strong nation;

Just building a super gleaming & dazzling nation
is all our notion,

Loving my mother India is my passion
of steadfast realization.

Meaning:-

1. *Creation:- the action or process of bringing something into existence.*

2. *Toleration:- the practice of tolerating something, in particular differences of opinion or behaviour.*

3. *Protection:- the action of protecting, or the state of being protected.*

4. *Nation :- country*

5. *Ambition:- aim, goal*

6. *Notion:- a conception of or belief about something.*

7. *Realization:- an act of becoming fully aware of something as a fact.*

46. Memorable Mistakes

Memorable mistakes, unforgettable wrangles,

Non-renewable smiles, fake talks;

Why all these things are happening?

Why all these things are battling?

We learn and forget the morals in life,

Our absurd behavior makes us feel great,

Unnecessary abuse, undiplomatic signs;

Make an appearance in this movie called life!

Slaking the lofty acts,

Abashing about joyful acts;

Abandoning the positive thoughts,

Abducting all the negative thoughts;

The unnecessary things become highly necessary,

The necessary things become unnecessary;

Oh lord! Is all your playful game.

Since it's all your playful game so all of us you do tame.

Meaning:-

1.   Tame:- protect n prepare us for life

47. Mother Cosmos

Out bursting life is my mother enchantment,
Entire cosmos is her signature is all her attainment;
But for laziness & procrastination she is an abolishment;
And for all the difficulties & hurdles she is not abandonment,
When it comes to songs she is a melody queen
of accomplishment,
Her achievements are so vast there is
no need for acknowledgement,
Give a look at her in every field she highlights achievement;
Her patience & tolerance! What not is her attainment!
All her selfless achievements for us is a bestowment,
Meditates for entire cosmos's betterment!
For all she is an angel of compliment,
She is an open book of concealment;
Joy doubles in her presence my mother enjoyment,
Of great knowledge and wisdom she is a big department;
Witty by nature obliterating muffness and impairment,
Whole cosmos is her family of great involvement;
A super strong lady of disillusionment,
Whole cosmos is her super embodiment;
She is a realized lady of great enlightenment,
All our wishes and desires she is a fulfillment;

Everywhere she spreads joy & leaks merriment,

To her I bow down is my steadfast happy statement.

Meaning:-

1. *Enchantment:- a feeling of great pleasure; delight.*

2. *Attainment:- the action or fact of achieving a goal towards which one has worked*

3. *Abolishment:- to officially end or stop (something, such as a law)*

4. *Abandonment:- the action or fact of abandoning or being abandoned.*

5. *Accomplishment:- something that has been achieved successfully.*

6. *Acknowledgement:- acceptance of the truth or existence of something.*

7. *Achievement:- success*

8. *Attainment:- the act of conferring an honor or presenting a gift.*

9. *Bestowement:- the act of conferring an honor or presenting a gift.*

10. *Betterment:- the improvement of something.*

11. *Compliment:- a polite expression of praise or admiration.*

12. *Concealment:- the action of hiding something or preventing it from being known.*

13. *Enjoyment:- the state or process of taking pleasure in something.*

14. *Department:- factory*

15. *Impairment:- the state or fact of a faculty or function being weakened or damaged.*

16. Involvement:- the fact or condition of being involved with or participating in something.

17. Disillutionment:- a feeling of disappointment resulting from the discovery that something is not as good as one believed it to be.

18. Embodiment:- a tangible or visible form of an idea, quality, or feeling.

19. Enlightenment:- a tangible or visible form of an idea, quality, or feeling.

20. Fulfillment:- a feeling of happiness and satisfaction

21. Merriment:- joy

22. Statement:- a definite or clear expression of something in speech or writing.

48. Do Seek

In severe worry don't distraught,

Oh the high minded one you are haught;

Bring out the moral values that are sought,

And then don't presume that you are a naught;

On the tip of success ladder you are already raught,

During the party do not excessively waught;

Remember that you are on watch,

Share all the lessons that are taught;

Day and night for truth & justice we together have fought.

Meaning:-

1. Distraught:- very upset & worried.

2. Haught:- Noble

3. Sought:- past sentence of seek

4. Naught:- Nothing

5. Raught:- past sentence of reach

6. Waught:- to drink deep

7. Fought: to quarrel

8. Taught:- to preach

49. Simple Motivation

During the pathway of growing strong,

Make new mistakes & learn for a life long;

Go join the master's playful song,

Enjoy every second say not 'I am wrong';

While standing on the success ladder don't be headlong,

Always think to entire universe you belong;

Let joy speak in your every stride of furlong,

**Oh master you are along and along you are
among and among!!!**

Meaning:-

1. *Strong:- mighty*

2. *Life long:- for entire life*

3. *Song:- a short poem or other set of words set to music or meant to be sung*

4. *Wrong:- a mistake*

5. *Headlong:- with the head foremost.*

6. *Belong:- be the property of*

7. *Furlong:- : a unit of distance equal to 220 yards (about 201 meters)*

8. *Among:- : in company or association with*

50. Echo of Silence

Let your universal message become prevalent,

For sure far aren't the days of enlightenment!!!

Don't wait but create the days of joy & excitement;

And all your achievements become an
inspiring encouragement;

Yes anger & impatience will surely lead to misjudgment-

Don't be adamant but be open for adjustment,

Your every action should lead to dazzlement-

Why welcome indonent & sleep & be complacent;

Long is life's journey so do things with commitment,

All your innovative ideas lead to holistic development-

Don't lose your heart due to the arrival of vanquishment;

And if at all you live, live like a leader
of decisive procurement-

Helping the poor & needy in action
be your humble pronouncement,

Your purpose of doing things happily be your
everyday advertisement;

Valuing time as its prime be your everyday's
foremost commencement.

Meaning:-

1.   Prevalent:-widespread

2. *Enlightenment:- give (someone) spiritual knowledge or insight, give (someone) greater knowledge and understanding about a subject or situation.*

3. *Overachiaevemant:- an excessive or unusually high level of achievement.*

4. *Excitement:- a feeling of great enthusiasm and eagerness.*

5. *Misjudgement:- the action of forming a wrong opinion or conclusion about something.*

6. *Adjustment:- a small alteration or movement made to achieve a desired fit, appearance, or result.*

7. *Dazzlement:- good impression*

    Complacent:- showing smug or uncritical satisfaction with oneself or one›s achievements.

8. *Commitment:- the state or quality of being dedicated to a cause, activity, etc.*

9. *Vanquishment:- defeating thoroughly.*

10. *Commencement:- the beginning of something.*

11. *Advertizement:-promotion*

12. *Pronouncement:-An announcement*

13. *Expungement:- obliterate or remove completely (something unwanted or unpleasant).*

14. *Decisive:- having or showing the ability to make decisions quickly and effectively.*

15. *Procurement:- obtaining especially with care or effort.*

51. Fact

Dare not suffer in insufficiency,

Why not drip in an innate esctacy?

Increase your creativity of fantacy;

No matter what, hit back of bouncy;

Increasing the accuracy of our efficacy;

Endlessly spread knowledge in vibrancy,

Ruling entire universe in a dignified legacy,

So let open the doors of your success agency,

Enjoy the entire life in the mode of buoyancy;

Realise whole universe as our own constituency,

You remind oneself that you are no more in infancy;

The honest efforts behind achievement is the secrecy,

We belong to human race let that be the prominency;

In your work & action highlight competency;

Why weakly confess in inconsistency,

Just focus on increasing your proficiency.

Meaning:-

1. Insufficiency:- the condition of being insufficient, lack of

2. Ecstasy:- an overwhelming feeling of great happiness or joyful excitement.

3. Fantasy:- the faculty or activity of imagining impossible or improbable things.

4. *Bouncy:- bouncing or causing things to bounce.*

5. *Efficacy:- the power to produce a desired result*

6. *Vibrancy:- the state of being full of energy and life.*

7. *Legacy:- a gift by will especially of money or other personal property*

8. *Agency:- a business or organization providing a particular service on behalf of another business, person, or group.*

9. *Consistency:- regularity*

10. *Infancy:- the state or period of babyhood or early childhood.*

11. *Secrecy:- the action of keeping something secret or the state of being kept secret.*

12. *Prominency:- the state of being important, famous, or noticeable.*

13. *Competency:- the ability to do something successfully or efficiently.*

14. *Inconsistency:- irregularity*

15. *Proficiency:- : advancement in knowledge or skill : Progress*

52. Worth Knowing

Don't be ignorant & lazily lenient,

But for elders and guru be obedient;

Inner beauty matters which is salient,

Hey hang on! my pal, you don't reorient;

You stay cool, stay balanced and be patient,

And let your focus speak from time ancient;

Failures are not permanent they are transient,

Growing nation strong be the mantra of salient;

Dare not say I am fragile in the mode of nescient,

Wittily encounter the difficulties and be resilient;

Be exuberantly on for knowledge you be esurient,

With bubbling boiling enthusiasm be ebullient;

Fight all inner foes by being self-sufficient.

Meaning:-

1. *Reorient:- change the focus or direction of.*

2. *Patient:- able to accept or tolerate delays, problems, or suffering without becoming annoyed or anxious.*

3. *Ancient:- belonging to the very distant past and no longer in existence.*

4. *Salient:- important*

5. *Lenient:- (of a punishment or person in authority) more merciful or tolerant than expected.*

6. *Obedient:- complying or willing to comply with an order or request; submissive to another's authority.*

7. *Transient:- lasting only for a short time; impermanent.*

8. *Nescient:- lacking knowledge; ignorant.*

9. *Resilent:- (of a person or animal) able to withstand or recover quickly from difficult conditions.*

10. *Ensurient:- hungry or greedy*

11. *Ebbulient:- cheerful and full of energy.*

12. *Self-sufficient:- independent, needing no outside help in satisfying one's basic needs, especially with regard to the production of food.*

53. Swami Vivekananda

A bright scintillating flash of inspiration,

A true lover of India, his mother nation;

For his every act, people praise in ovation,

He is extremely brilliant is the realization;

A super spiritual giant of great motivation,

A wandering guru spreading great affirmation,

A universal guru of high and great admiration;

A meditative master, who is mastery in concentration,

Who is blest with his master's blessings and protection;

To all his believers & devotees he is a strong foundation-

A truly enchanting simple guru of high reputation,

He lives for others, what a fantastic notion;

Writing and studying is his innate passion,

Very popular for his elocution & oration.

Pranams to you oh Guru is all the actualization.

Meaning:-

1. *Inspiration:- the process of being mentally stimulated to do or feel something, especially to do something creative.*

2. *Nation:- Country*

3. *Ovation:- a sustained and enthusiastic show of appreciation from an audience, especially by means of applause.*

4. *Realisation:- an act of becoming fully aware of something as a fact.*

5.   *Motivation:- an internal state that propels individuals to engage in goal-directed behavior.*

6.   *Affirmation:- the act or an instance of affirming; state of being affirmed.*

7.   *Concentration:- the action or power of focusing all one's attention.*

8.   *Foundation:- an organization that has been created in order to provide money for a particular group of people in need of help or for a particular type of study*

9.   *Reputation:- the opinion that people in general have about someone or something, or how much respect or admiration someone or something receives, based on past behaviour or character*

10.   *Notion:- a belief or idea:*

11.   *Elocuation:- the art of careful public speaking, using clear pronunciation and good breathing to control the voice*

12.   *Oration:- a formal public speech about a serious subject*

13.   *Passion:- a very powerful feeling*

54. Live the Life's Game

Hey you dance joyfully to the rhythm of rain,

Spread exuberance everywhere again and again;

Don't ignorantly in folly you joyfully do remain,

Such you spread the wit, all the foolishness should drain;

The knowledge from every corner of this universe you obtain,

You must regain the lost charm you regain you regain;

But for oneself in vain in pain don't strain,

Learn, Lead & love everyone be the life's game.

Meaning:-

1. *Rain:- the condensed moisture of the atmosphere falling visibly in separate drops.*

2. *Again:- the condensed moisture of the atmosphere falling visibly in separate drops.*

3. *Remain:- continue to exist, especially after other similar people or things have ceased to do so*

4. *Drain:- cause the water or other liquid in (something) to run out, leaving it empty or dry.*

5. *Obtain:- get, acquire, or secure (something).*

6. *Regain:- obtain possession or use of (something, typically a quality or ability) again after losing it.*

7. *Strain:- cause great effort*

8. *Game:- playful activity, an activity that one engages in for amusement or fun.*

55. Inspiration

Ignite the light of your mind temple,

Such you live that people take your example;

Let the solution for every hard question be very simple,

Spread all the love and affection in enormous ample;

Outgrow the difficulties don't at all cripple,

Long life's journey don't trip and popple;

All the negations you crush & crumple.

**With a devotional insight impress
every person all the people!!!**

Meaning:-

1. *Temple:- a building for religious worship.*

2. *Example:- instance.*

3. *Simple:- not complex and complicated.*

4. *Ample:- enough or more than enough; plentiful.*

5. *Cripple:- cause severe and disabling damage to; deprive of the ability to function normally.*

6. *Popple:- to lift or haul (something heavy) with great effort.*

7. *Crumple:- crush (something, typically paper or cloth) so that it becomes creased and wrinkled.*

56. Durgamba my Possibility

I do actually & always endorse the patience,
commitment & priority

But an intense & Creativity in every act
was seen of immensity

Very enthusiastic by nature she was an optimist in reality

In each & every act in abundance was seen possibility

An all-embracing character out bursting spirituality

Is all she was underlining in the mode of humility

My favorite mother is super honest of sincerity

Always promoting possibility of innate clarity

Every-time highlighting the quality of charity

Sheer generosity, authenticity, and felicity.

All work she does it handy but in ingenuity

Logical lady without confusion & no ambiguity

Is all my truly encouraging mother in actuality

My mother of fair complexity is my mother of true ability

She is my mother of richness out bursting wealth & prosperity

But for knowledge and yogic wisdom
is my mother of total clarity

I say ambaa ambaa feels like heaven
is on earth experiencing clarity

My truly loving and adoring mother
singing shambo in reality

Meaning:-

1. *Patience:-* the capacity to accept or tolerate delay, problems, or suffering without becoming annoyed or anxious.

2. *Commitment:-* the capacity to accept or tolerate delay, problems, or suffering without becoming annoyed or anxious.

3. *Priority:-* the fact or condition of being regarded or treated as more important than others

4. *Immensity:-* of a big amount

5. *Optimist:-* the extremely large size, scale, or extent of something.

6. *Reality:-* the fact

7. *Possibility:-* the state or fact of being possible; likelihood.

8. *Spirituality:-* Spirituality involves the recognition of a feeling or sense or belief that there is something greater than myself, something more to being human than sensory experience, and that the greater whole of which we are part is cosmic or divine in nature.

9. *Humility:-* the quality of having a modest or low view of one's importance.

10. *Sincerity:-* being honest

11. *Clarity:-* the quality of being coherent and intelligible.

12. *Felicity:-* intense happiness.

13. *Ingenuinity:-* the quality of being clever, original, and inventive.

14. *Ambiguity:- confusion*

15. *Actuality:- reality*

16. *Ability:-capability*

17. *Prosperity:- the condition of being successful or thriving*

18. *Reality:- Actuality*

19. *Enterity:- as a whole*

57. Learning Lessons!

Once you work towards the proficiency,

Let all your efforts be full of consistency;

All your goals you reach in full competency;

Thus naturally you will be a success agency,

All your linguistic capability be full of innate fluency,

By then don't be ignorant in urgency;

In your entire legacy be known for decency,

Oh the strong gusto you be full of potency.

Meaning:-

1. *Proficiency:- fluency.*

2. *Competency:- the ability to do something successfully or efficiently.*

3. *Agency:- company, organization.*

4. *Consistency:- regularity.*

5. *Fluency:- the quality or condition of being fluent.*

6. *Urgency:- importance requiring swift action.*

7. *Decency:- behaviour that conforms to accepted standards of morality or respectability.*

8. *Potency:- the power of something to influence or make an impression.*

58. Play

There is no beginning no doomsday,

Entire cosmos is our master's play;

Always in joyful mood you do stay,

Past is an yesterday so you live for today;

Whether its horseplay or swordplay-

Exuberantly live in every way,

Let any hurdle come on my pathway;

Fight it all with courage on each and every day!

But for negations you obliterate and slay!

Dare not howl and run far far away;

In vain in pain don't at all bray,

Spread love, peace and joy not affray,

Let your every stride add on to your hay day;

Walk straight towards your goal not astray;

When everyway is blind you outgrow the light ray,

Let your strength & positivity speak not in dismay,

Clarity in every action whether mid-day or sky-way,

Outwit every challenge & win this life say hooray!!

Think that everyday is a new day, everyday is a payday,

For each and every hurdle you
giving solutions be the keyway;

Don't while away time & be lazy in the homestay,

Let every moment you inspire the entire day;
You are born to motivate all in every pathway,
Every second is yours execute it playfully is all I say;
Live life so well that people call you route way,
If you are wisdomlessly techie,
for sure it leads to doom in every way;
All the inborn talent you just display,
Joyfully arise that every day is a holiday;
But for achievement & learning let open the doorway,
Don't at all run away you face the raceway;
Week day or week end day on everyday be the headway,
Outplay! You just outplay!
One day you will reach the ultimate way,
Why in strife say I can't and lazily hide & stay in a sickbay;
When every day is a playful day joyfully
sing & dance with goombay,
When every situation you take care
entire life is your game day,
Say yes to life, yes to love, Yes to lead a joyful day;
Workday or workout day let every day be a perky day,
Enjoy your every pathway whether its
walk way or walk away;
Stay alive, stay attentive, and just be faraway,
Think new solutions increase your creativity and make this
life a colorful way.

Meaning:-

1. *Doomsday:- a time of catastrophic destruction and death*
2. *Play:- engage in activity for enjoyment and recreation rather than a serious or practical purpose.*
3. *Stay:- remain in the same place.*
4. *Today:- on or in the course of this present day.*
5. *Swordplay:- the activity or skill of fencing with swords or foils.*
6. *Way:- a road, track, or path for travelling along.*
7. *Pathway:- A pathway is a trail or other walkway*
8. *Everyday:- happening or used every day; daily.*
9. *Slay:- kill, destroy*
10. *Away:- to or at a distance from a particular place, person, or thing.*
11. *Bray:- the loud, harsh cry of a donkey or mule.*
12. *Affray:- fight, battle*
13. *Day:- each of the twenty-four-hour periods, reckoned from one midnight to the next, into which a week, month, or year is divided, and corresponding to a rotation of the earth on its axis.*
14. *Astray:- away from the correct path or direction.*
15. *Heyday:- the period of a person's or thing's greatest success, popularity, activity, or vigour.*
16. *Light ray:- The light traveling in any one direction in a straight line*
17. *Dismay:- concern and distress caused by something unexpected.*
18. *Midday:- afternoon*
19. *Skyway:- a recognized route followed by aircraft.*
20. *Hooray:- used to express joy or approval.*

21. *Payday:-* the day of the week or month on which you receive your wages or salary.

22. *Keyway:-* a slot cut in a part of a machine or an electrical connector, to ensure correct orientation with another part which is fitted with a key.

23. *Homestay:-* a form of hospitality and lodging whereby visitors share a residence with a local of the area (host) to which they are traveling.

24. *Say:-* utter words so as to convey information, an opinion, a feeling or intention, or an instruction.

25. *Display:-* put (something) in a prominent place in order that it may readily be seen.

26. *Holiday:-* an extended period of leisure and recreation, especially one spent away from home or in travelling.

27. *Doorway:-* an entrance to a room or building through a door.

28. *Raceway:-* an enclosed conduit that forms a physical pathway for electrical wiring

29. *Headway:-* forward movement of a ship or boat, especially when this is slow or difficult.

30. *Sickbay:-* an area, especially on a ship or navy base, or in Britain in a school or university, where medical treatment is given and where beds are provided for people who are ill

31. *Goombay:-* a goatskin drum with a round or squared top, played with the hands.

32. *Gameday:-* The day on which a sports team plays a game.

33. *Walkaway:-* an easy victory or conquest

34. *Faraway:-* distant in space or time.

35. *Colourful way:-* a combination of colours or one particular colour in which something such as clothing, cloth, or paper is made, or in which a place is decorated.

59. Frank Expression

Tears and tears of esctacy and devotion,

Heart felt pranams and veneration;

Innate candidness & satisfaction,

In my every birth I have your promised protection;

Positivity breading machine be your invention,

Decimate negation with determination;

Don't accept that you are an imperfect fraction,

Happily think that whole universe is your mansion;

Charity should begin at home so first serve mother nation.

Meaning:-

1. *Esctacy:- an overwhelming feeling of great happiness or joyful excitement.*

2. *Devotion:- bhakti*

3. *Veneration:- great respect; reverence.*

4. *Candidness:- the quality of being open, honest, or straightforward*

5. *Satisfaction:- meet the expectations, needs, or desires of (someone).*

6. *Protection:- the action of protecting, or the state of being protected.*

7. *Invention:- the action of inventing something, typically a process or device.*

8.   *Determination:- the quality of being determined; firmness of purpose.*

9.   *Fraction:- a numerical quantity that is not a whole number (e.g. 1/2, 0.5).*

10.   *Mansion:-home*

11.   *Nation:- country*

60. Mother Serenity

Her innate patience is but enormous;

In her every do she is but adventurous,

Teaches entire cosmos my mother famous,

Cool and composed is my mother equanimous,

Sweet and sugary lady is she my mother pious;

But for injustice & terror she is deadly venomous;

But if at all she is angry everything seems disastrous,

She says follow the path of difficulty fear not for hazardous;

She and her mastery in every subject
which is simply fantabulous;

She is philliantrophic by nature is my mother generous,

In her presence all our weakness & pain vanishes;

This witty lady makes us knowledge ravenous,

Every second every moment be joyous,

In everything is her signature oh my mother fantabulous.

Meaning:-

1. *Serenity:- the state of being calm, peaceful, and untroubled.*

2. *Enormous:- very large in size, quantity, or extent.*

3. *Adventourous:- willing to take risks or to try out new methods, ideas, or experiences.*

4. *Famous:- Popular*

5. *Equanimous:- calm and composed.*

6.   *Pious:- soft*

7.   *Venomous:- poisonous*

8.   *Disastrous:- causing great damage.*

9.   *Hazardous:- risky; dangerous.*

10.   *Fantabulous:- excellent; wonderful.*

11.   *Generous:- showing a readiness to give more of something, especially money, than is strictly necessary or expected.*

12.   *Vanishes:- disappear suddenly and completely.*

13.   *Ravenous:- extremely hungry.*

14.   *Joyous:- happy*

15.   *Fantabulous:- fantastic*

61. Cold & Bold is my Hanuman I Told

Be like my master the super infallible,

He the bold, he the cold, he is Mr. Possible.

Everywhere every time his happy face is probable;

He, witty super human for him nothing is impossible,

Anywhere n everywhere you are visible oh my admirable,

Whether I m a buzzing bee or on the
tree you are my adorable,

Your highly matured benevolent acts are
highly highly acceptable;

Ur limitless knowledge and charming presence is exceptionally
remarkable.

Oh the pleasurable, oh the amiable your marvelous
contributions is truly incredible truly incredible.

Meaning:-

1. Infallible:- never failing; always effective.

2. Possible:- able to be done or achieved.

3. Probable:- most likely

4. Impossible:- not possible

5. Admirable:- arousing or deserving respect and approval.

6. Adorable:- inspiring great affection or delight.

7. Acceptible:- able to be agreed on; suitable.

8. Remarkable:- worthy of attention; striking.

9. Incredible:- impossible to believe., unique extraordinary to
believe

62. My Teach

Don't regret that you are an incomplete soul?

Why in vain and pain ferociously insanely howl?

In this life's playful drama you joyfully perform your role:

Work upon to decrease population explosion
in your status sole,

By wiping the tears of the weeping and
crying hearts be your life's goal,

Engross yourself in a meditative realm
and from within you ensoul,

Respect mother nature's free gifts never at all be foul;

Live like a universal citizen on the whole,

Exterminate sorrow in all and console;

Give a soothing touch to all the lives don't at all troll.

Meaning:-

1. Soul:- the spiritual or immaterial part of a human being or
    animal, regarded as immortal.

2. Howl:- a long, doleful cry uttered by an animal such as a
    dog or wolf.

3. Role:- an actor's part in a play, film, etc

4. Sole:- one and only one

5. Goal:- aim

6. Ensoul:- endow with a soul

7.   *Foul:- able to repel a particular thing; impervious to a particular substance.*

8.   *Whole:- all of; entire.*

9.   *Console:- comfort (someone) at a time of grief or disappointment.*

10. *Troll:- a person who intentionally antagonizes others online by posting inflammatory, irrelevant, or offensive comments or other disruptive content.*

63. A Request

Don't suffer in woe,

And sadly feel low;

From head till tip toe,

Let your exuberance flow:

Just keep up the glow;

Fear not your foe,

Leak joy in every show:

To be a fullfledged one you grow,

So you simply GROW, GROW and GROW.

Meaning:-

1.   Woe:- great sorrow or distress (often used hyperbolically).

64. Learn from Life!!!

Stay in a firm mode of simplicity,

Don't dissolve in susceptibility,

During worship, you be full of divinity:

Why suffer in the realm of impossibility?

Instead let open the doors of your ability,

Don't demand but command high respectability;

Live like entire universe is your territoriality;

And among inter & intra-community
spread the lessons of integrity,

Boldly spread the notion "Unity in diversity"

Sell your wit in the mode of intellectuality,

Live happily in harmony and compatibility;

Don't give rooms for stupidity,

Every day & in every moment
you leave behind new possibility,

Such you fortify all that there is no place for disability;

Don't conclude that you are a fragility,

Grow, grow and grow of immensity;

Let your patience be full of availability,

Take fab decisions of steadfast capability;

Err is to human of infallibility,

Not repeating the mistakes be the mentality;

Welcome the wisdom in admissibility,
Don't let the negations conquer you in perplexity;
With innate joy you lead everyone not in aridity,
Puke possibility and creativity,
Enjoy the life to its fullest capacity;
During worship you deeply meditate on your universal deity,
Spread the lessons of purity in verity,
Invite possibility to your fullest ability;
You outgrow the wittiest and the mightiest in reality.

Meaning:-

1. *Impossibility:- that which is not possible*

2. *Ability:- possession of the means or skill to do something.*

3. *Respectability:- the quality of being socially acceptable.*

4. *Simplicity:- the quality or condition of being easy to understand or do.*

5. *Divinity:- the state or quality of being divine.*

6. *Susceptibility:- the quality or state of being exposed to the possibility of being attacked or harmed, either physically or emotionally.*

7. *Territoriality:- persistent attachment to a specific territory.*

8. *Integrity:- the quality of being honest and having strong moral principles.*

9. *Diversity:- the state of being diverse; variety.*

10. *Intellectuality:- intellectual character or power.*

11. *Compatibility:- a feeling of sympathy and friendship; like-mindedness.*

12. *Stupidity:-* behaviour that shows a lack of good sense or judgement.

13. *Possibility:-* the state or fact of being possible; likelihood.

14. *Disability:-* a physical or mental condition that limits a person's movements, senses, or activities.

15. *Fragility:-* the quality of being easily broken or damaged.

16. *Immensity:-* the extremely large size, scale, or extent of something.

17. *Availability:-* to be present available.

18. *Capability:-* the power or ability to do something.

19. *Infallibility:-* quality of being incapable of making mistakes or being wrong.

20. *Mentality:-* the characteristic way of thinking of a person or group.

21. *Admissibility:-* the quality of being acceptable or valid, especially as evidence in a court of law.

22. *Perplexity:-* confusion.

23. *Aridity:-* the state of not being interesting or successful.

24. *Creativity:-* innovative and unique ideas.

25. *Capacity:-* the maximum amount that something can contain and is able.

26. *Diety:-* a god or goddess (in a polytheistic religion).

27. *Verity:-* a true principle or belief, especially one of fundamental importance.

28. *Ability:-* be capable of.

29. *Reality:-* real life, actuality.

65. Hanuman the Doom Master!!!

He is an enlightened master of longevity,

Who thinks in the mode of rationality;

A rare combination of wit and might is the actuality,

Everyone in joy & wonder say "what a personality!!!"

He is a composition of masculine and femininity,

He is a ruling king of super possibility;

He is balanced focused full of stability,

But for negation he is hyper resistivity;

A king of knowledge and humility,

Pragmatic master of high sensitivity;

His entire brain is a huge holistic university,

Big thinks he leaks in the mode of simplicity;

In his entire presence there is no inequality.

No disability, no perplexity, everywhere is truth and unlimited exuberant possibility!!!

Meaning:-

1. Longevity:- Long life.

2. Rationality:- the quality of being based on or in accordance with reason or logic.

3. Actuality:- the state of existing in reality.

4. Personality:- the combination of characteristics or qualities that form an individual's distinctive character.

5. *Femininity:- qualities or attributes regarded as characteristic of women or girls.*

6. *Possibility:- a thing that may be chosen or done out of several possible alternatives.*

7. *Stability:- the state of being stable.*

8. *Resistivity:- a measure of the resisting power of a specified material to the flow of an electric current.*

9. *Humility:- the quality of having a modest or low view of one's importance.*

10. *Sensitivity:- the quality or condition of being sensitive.*

11. *University:- a high-level educational institution in which students study for degrees and academic research is done.*

12. *Simplicity:- the state of being simple, uncomplicated, or uncompounded. : lack of subtlety or penetration : innocence, naiveté : folly, silliness. 3. : freedom from pretense or guile : candor.*

13. *Inequality:- difference in size, degree, circumstances, etc.; lack of equality.*

66. Philosophy of Life

Joyfully dance to the rhythm of life,

Suffer not in agony suffer not in strife;

Jump! Beat the drums! And playfully play the fife,

Make your life's journey a joyful one, all positives you rife;

Oh the brilliant one you are born to achieve in this life-

Hurdles come hurdles go it's all a phase of life,

Whether its birds or animals respect the wildlife;

Let it be a show life or show off life you be full of high life.

Meaning:-

1. Fife:- a kind of small shrill flute used with the drum in military bands.

67. Hie Towards Growth

Ignite the inner spiritual beacon fire,

But for all negations you just gun fire;

Long is life's journey so you simply aspire,

In every step, in every stride you just inspire:

Such you motivate all that people will just admire,

You aim big things in life for petty don't crave cry & tire,

Such you live oh the legendary,
let not your motivation expire.

You exterminate the pangs of sorrow & all the
momentary desire.

68. Super Lessons

Why shamefully sink in imbecility,

From all command respectability;

You be the owner of the witty city,

Forget not to teach the lessons of unity;

You worship bhajrang the universal diety,

But for poor & ruth show compassion and pity;

Rest leave it to god and live with compatibility-

Trust you show with your innate strength and ability.

Meaning:-

1. Imbecility:- being very stupid or foolish

2. Compatibility:- a state in which two things are able to exist or occur together without problems or conflict.

69. Ostentatious Har

Highly meditative in every sit,

Of yogic body he is highly fit;

Famous for his scintillating wit,

Known as our silent master isn't it?

Spreads joyful smile on every git;

Very adventurous & traveling spirit,

While facing the hurdles he never quit;

He is a motivational guide of a strong hit,

His inspiring speeches have no limit;

Yes a soft hearted man I admit,

A scholarly man I truly accept it;

His lexicon power has no ambit,

Innovative visions he emit!

He is only my master of the end I just can feel it.

Meaning:-

1. *Scintillating:- shining brightly.*

2. *Git:- an unpleasant or contemptible person.*

3. *Spirit:- the non-physical part of a person which is the seat of emotions and character; the soul.*

4. *Ambit:- the scope, extent, or bounds of something.*

70. *Vivacious Mother!!!*

A lady of richness and prosperity;

A truly flawless lady outbursting purity,

Drives me crazy by her logical sentimentality;

Look at her focused and committed ability;

Her every action depicts dignified responsibility,

Here comes my mother a fountain head of spirituality,

Always she is worshipping shambo of immensity;

Queen of devotion is my mother tolerability,

At times brahmacharini, mother of chastity;

Sometimes she is the mother of immortality,

Immensely affectionate is my mother yoga entity;

If at all I love its this mother to her entirety,

She is well known for generosity & charity;

Looking at her briny of knowledge & wisdom
I am inspired is the actuality,

Meaning:-

1. *Spirituality:- the quality of being concerned with the human spirit or soul as opposed to material or physical things.*

2. *Ability:- the quality of being concerned with the human spirit or soul as opposed to material or physical things.*

3. *Responsibility:- something that it is your job or duty to deal with:*

4. *Sentimentality:-Strongly influenced by emotional feelings.*

5. *Purity:- freedom from adulteration or contamination.*

6. *Immensity:- the extremely large size, scale, or extent of something.*

7. *Tolerability:- capable to suffer patiently.*

8. *Chastity:- virginity.*

9. *Immortality:- the quality or state of being immortal.*

10. *Prosperity:- The state of being prosperous.*

11. *Actuality:- the state of existing in reality.*

12. *Entity:- a thing with distinct and independent existence.*

13. *Charity:- an organization set up to provide help and raise money for those in need.*

14. *Entirety:- the whole of something.*

71. Say Yes to Life!

Why blame your irony of fate,

Don't do things that you always hate;

And stay not timid is all I state,

Just do things jauntily and be accurate;

Don't boast oneself and exaggerate,

And realize the power of possibility & tolerate;

Of super great visions you just update,

With an inspirational blend you debate;

Bring out soaring ideas from within thoughtfully innate,

Let your ego and laziness just ablate;

We belong to human race so don't discriminate,

Your qualities of positivity you just differentiate;

Obliterate negations by your firm take,

But for patience & wit from within you just regenerate;

Ignite the light in all which is but a necessitate,

For which you must know how to focus & concentrate;

False believes & superstitions do exist which is unfortunate,

Think logical be practical & participate;

In this competitive life you got to be wise & illustrate,

That you are a great capability with an expiry date;

Each & every work you do it with joy, oh my passionate,

With lots of positivity you just joyfully reverberate.

Meaning:-

1. *Fate:- the development of events outside a person's control, regarded as predetermined by a supernatural power.*

2. *Hate:- feel intense dislike for.*

3. *State:- the particular condition that someone or something is in at a specific time.*

4. *Jauntily:- in a way that shows that you are happy and confident.*

5. *Accurate:- correct, exact, and without any mistakes.*

6. *Exaggerate:- represent (something) as being larger, better, or worse than it really is.*

7. *Tolerate:- allow the existence, occurrence, or practice of (something that one dislikes or disagrees with) without interference.*

8. *Update:- make (something) more modern or up to date.*

9. *Debate:- argue about (a subject), especially in a formal manner.*

10. *Innate:- inborn.*

11. *Abate:- (of something unpleasant or severe) become less intense or widespread.*

12. *Discriminate:- make an unjust or prejudicial distinction in the treatment of different categories of people, especially on the grounds of ethnicity, sex, age, or disability.*

13. *Differentiate:- recognize or ascertain what makes (someone or something) different.*

14. *Regenerate:- (of a living organism) grow (new tissue) after loss or damage.*

15. *Necessitate:- make (something) necessary as a result or consequence.*

16. *Concentrate:- focus all one's attention on a particular object or activity.*

17. *Unfortunate:- having or marked by bad fortune; unlucky*

18. *Participate:- take part in an action or endeavour.*

19. *Illustrate:- provide (a book, newspaper, etc.) with pictures.*

20. *Date:- the day of the month or year as specified by a number.*

21. *Passionate:- having, showing, or caused by strong feelings or beliefs.*

22. *Reverberate:- (of a loud noise) be repeated several times as an echo.*

72. My Ineffable Mother!!!

She was truely a doting mother & a symbol of amity,
In her every presence everywhere is truth & prosperity;
Devotingly worshipping shambo of immensity,
Tears of ecstasy flows from her eyes is the actuality;
This lady is for always outbursting in femininity,
Shambo was her strength & master of great affinity;
This universal teacher was inspiring
all in the mode of simplicity,
Big and soaring innovative visions
she leaks my lady of super capability;
Known for affection & generosity is my mother tolerability,
A lady of solutions obliterating complexity;
She bows down to trinity of gods with intense humility,
She commands respect in her every act of dignity;
Prosperity seen everywhere eradicating paucity,
A blemish less lady promotes & supports unity and integrity;
Her every action portrays intense responsibility,
Even before hurdles come she can foresee with certainty;
Protecting & gaurding all of us were her outrageous quality,
Dissolves all of us in the pool of her sweet,
caring sentimentality;
Inspiring & highly motivational she is, is all her ability,

She is holistically a strong lady exterminating cecity;

Balances the entire cosmos with high compatibility,

This universal lady leaks immensely the purity;

**So I bow down with sheer humility
to this mother of possibility!!!**

Meaning:-

1. *Amity:- friendly relations.*

2. *Prosperity:- the state of being prosperous.*

3. *Immensity:- the extremely large size, scale, or extent of something.*

4. *Actuality:- the state of existing in reality.*

5. *femininity:- qualities or attributes regarded as characteristic of women or girls.*

6. *Affinity:- a close similarity between two things, or an attraction or sympathy for someone or something, esp. because of shared characteristics.*

7. *Simplicity:- the quality or condition of being easy to understand or do.*

8. *Capability:- the power or ability to do something.*

9. *Tolerability:- able to be endured.*

10. *Complexity:- the state or quality of being intricate or complicated.*

11. *Humility:- the quality of having a modest or low view of one's importance.*

12. *Dignity:- the state or quality of being worthy of honour or respect.*

13. *Paucity:-*

14. *Paucity:- the presence of something in only small or insufficient quantities or amounts.*

15. *Integrity:- the quality of being honest and having strong moral principles.*

16. *Responsibility:- the state or fact of having a duty to deal with something or of having control over someone.*

17. *Certainty:- firm conviction that something is the case.*

18. *Quality:- standard.*

19. *Sentimentality:- exaggerated and self-indulgent tenderness, sadness, or nostalgia.*

20. *Ability:- talent, skill, or proficiency in a particular area.*

21. *Cecity:- blindness.*

22. *Compatibility:- the natural ability to live or work together in harmony because of well-matched characteristics.*

23. *Purity:- the condition or quality of being pure; freedom from anything that debases, contaminates, pollutes, etc.*

24. *Possibility:- the state or fact of being possible:*

73. Words from Heart!!

You dont be very satisfied dear by the
mere desires that are momentary,

Long way ahead to grow oneself
so you outgrow all the visionary;

Now its high time to do things that are
highly highly necessary,

Lets grow our rich tradition and culture oh my sweet deary;

Dont say I am fragile & weak its a steadfast cautionary,

You are born to ignite light in all oh the legendary;

Help ruth, poor & needy by being voluntary,

Say not I am foolish say not I am weary;

Dont say I am an ordinary you are
born to be an extraordinary,

You are born to leak flamboyance in every
pathway oh my sweet sugary.

Meaning:-

1. *Momentary:- desires that stay for a short period of time.*

2. *Visionary:- thinking about or planning the future with imagination or wisdom.*

3. *Necessary:- needed to be done, achieved, or present; essential.*

4. *Deary:- darling.*

5. *Cautionary:- serving as a warning.*

6.   *Legendary:- remarkable enough to be famous; very well known.*

7.   *Voluntary:- done, given, or acting of one's own free will.*

8.   *Weary:- tired, exhausted.*

9.   *Extraordiunary:- not ordinary.*

10. *Flamboyance:- the tendency to attract attention because of one's exuberance, confidence, and stylishness.*

74. Ravishing Mother Exquisite

She is balancing on the tip of the acme of happiness,

Engrossed in chants, worship & meditativeness

She enjoys her every bit of aloofness,

She says "enjoy your every do with adeptness;

Beat the drums with aliveness,

So we shall sing & dance with all the mightiness;

Never complain in the mode of aimlessness,

Don't dissolve yourself in the pool of ambiguousness;

Knowingly why suffer in weakness,

Let your fortitude speak at peakness;

Hug the entire universe with inclusiveness,

Ignite the light of wisdom in all of brightness;

Let there be no rooms for confusion and laziness,

See everything in clarity not haziness;

Practice meditation even in aloneness,

She says "Be a giver of joy not sadness"

**Therefore she in all ignites the light of devotion &
knowledge of limitlessness!!!**

Meaning:-

1. Happiness:- joy

2. Meditativeness:- relating to or absorbed in meditation or considered thought.

3. *Aloofness:- not interested or involved socially.*

4. *Adeptness:- having a natural ability to do something that needs skill.*

5. *Aliveness:- with liveliness.*

6. *Mightiness:- of power*

7. *Aimlessness:- the condition of being without clear intentions, purpose, or direction:*

8. *Ambiguousness:- having or expressing more than one possible meaning, sometimes intentionally:*

9. *Weakness:- fragile.*

10. *Peakness:- at the highest top.*

11. *Inclusiveness:- the quality of including many different types of people and treating them all fairly and equally.*

12. *Brightness:- illumination.*

13. *Laziness:- the quality of not being willing to work or use any effort.*

14. *Haziness:- without clarity.*

15. *Sadness:- the condition or quality of being sad.*

16. *Limitnessness:- without end, limit, or boundary.*

75. Words of Alert!

Don't remorse in shame

Look this is just the master's game

Far is our true hame

Do give light like a flame

Don't go behind the fame

Just walk straight towards your aim

Don't say I am tired and lame

All hurdles you have overcame

Everywhere see your master's name

So is his game so is all his game.

Meaning:-

1.　Hame:- a Scots word for home.

76. Inspire

In the mode of quietitude,

With the breath of fortitude;

Of a sweet motivational attitude;

Helping the people of decreptitude,

With a strong notion of gratitude;

Never think in the mode of pulchritude,

Command respect of verisimilitude;

Have patience is but in plentitude,

Following devotional path be your habitude,

Stay highly focused in life that you forget senectitude;

Be so focused in life that you be a pathway of correctitude,

Just come out of the pool of inaptitude;

Day in and day out you increase your aptitude,

It's a steadfast caution don't stay in disquietude;

Be open for changes by vicissitude-

Be matured & decent in front of multitude.

Meaning:-

1. Quietitude:- a state of being calm and peaceful.

2. Fortitude:- courage over a long period.

3. Attitude:- the way you feel about something or someone, or a particular feeling or opinion:

4. *Decreptitude:- the fact of being in very bad condition because of being old, or not having been cared for, or having been used a lot.*

5. *Gratitude:- the feeling or quality of being grateful.*

6. *Pulchritude:- beauty, especially a woman's beauty*

7. *Verisimilitude:- the quality of seeming true or of having the appearance of being real.*

8. *Plentitude:- a full supply in abundance.*

9. *Habitude:- habit.*

10. *Senectitude:- the last stage of life.*

11. *Correctitude:- correctness, especially conscious correctness in one's behaviour.*

12. *Inaptitude:- lack of suitability or skill.*

13. *Aptitude:- a natural ability to do something.*

14. *Disquietitude:- a state of uneasiness or anxiety.*

15. *Vicissitude:- a change of circumstances or fortune, typically one that is unwelcome or unpleasant.*

16. *Multitude:- a large number of people or things.*

77. Guru Bajrang

Strength in all he instill:

A daring man of iron-will;

Lives a yoga freak up on the hill,

Exuberance in all he loves to fill,

With eyes closed he meditates until;

A silent thriller of unlimited strong will;

Till his master ram arrives, in the mode of still,

Loves and shares love without demanding bill,

He sings his lyrical poetry of infinite skill;

Drives everyone crazy by his out will,

In each and every one, joy he does fill;

All our dreams he will just full-fill,

Looking at this encyclopedia I in joy stand still;

On this pragmatic master recalling so I admire & chill.

Meaning:-

1. Instill:- fills
2. Outwill:- to demonstrate a stronger will than

78. We are What?

We are unique, we are an antique piece,
We are very special we the live like bees;
No matter we meditate every now and then:
But are rich at heart and fly with an ease.

We increase our involvement in work,
We always felt the heaven on this earth!
We have experienced the trips and falls,
We have also shed blood and tears at no loss-

We have revised the bad day's lessons everyday;
Have been correcting ourselves without any say:
We are born leaders and aim to rule;
Our state, our country, our world, our universe.

We have always been positive that we will reach our goal,
By fighting the hurdles with a strong and firm blow:
By then in the pathway we have mastered the art of patience;
The path of perseverance, the path of silence.

We take things easily and have worked smart in life,
And jump in pride with the lord's name
in our own special style:
We are totally devoted and have always been blessed;
To have been born to rule like the universe with pride!!!

79. Hanuman the Gaiety Master

Oh bhajrang I am mesmerized by your versatility of intellect,
A broadminded deity who always
earns & commands respect;

His every sentence is highly meaningful,
melodious & lyrical is all I detect,

In your firm stride confidence and strong will only reflect;

A great poet by nature an encyclopedia in every subject,

Highly focused in action out bursting
devotion in every aspect;

A delightful, exuberant & ineffable in every retrospect,

Soft at heart, big thinks in every path which I can't forget;

Serving with enthusiasm & wit,
oh bhajrang am I not correct?

"Every work you do, do it joyfully you say
with an emotional connect;

If at all I live its for you oh the ever
blazing spiritual firelight.

80. My only Master

Shady and peaceful enjoying solitude with pride,

He the famous tamer of souls known worldwide;

Oh the super spiritual master who else shall I abide?

You are known as universal master among nationwide!

Always you do worship hari/ram deity even on hill side,

You say "bring out the hidden talent
don't say & you don't hide",

Drops and drops of devoted tears were dribbling
from his eyes which he can't hide,

**Oh the epitome of devotion & strength you bow down to
your master in the mode of a devotional stride!**

81. Our Kingdom

All is silent, everything is still,

Everyone around to see the thrill!

Groves around dancing with gee;

I am the best said the busy bee;

Gracefully buzzing in a perky glee,

When roses and petals started to sing:

The leaves and the branches could not
stop beating the drums,

The budding flowers came with a flute and mic:

Questioning all the silent others
who never sang but kept quiet:

The hyper wind and the small hills;

Gave baground music & singing in their voice shill,

Generously, without even demanding bills in wonder,

Engrossed so much in their own world & carefully pondered;

Say clap sing loudly say we are the one:

Screaming lavishly in a high tone;

The seas and rivers gave a flexible dance,

Freely without demanding any allowance

Listen to the song go with the rhythm:

Melodiously sang the rocks like as though
it was their own written algorithm,

without missing this fortunate chance:

these butterflies were meditating in trance;

Stones sang clap clap clap from the beneath,

Jumping and singing perkily from far underneath:-

The frogs and fishes never gave up a chance:

By dancing every moment encouraging everyone & rance,

They behaved like as though they were the perfect audience!

These ducks and swans flew into
the sky in the language of silence,

They said fauntingly that they were very busy;

Watching the show the crocodiles were fizzy:-

Gossiping and munching the yummy snacks,

It reminds me of these human house wives:-

Said the same crocodiles with a taunt,

Foolishly reacting to the taunts;

How dare u the dark one!!!

"Take it easy don't u dare run"

It was the loudest voice from the far.

Its our king lion in burmudas:

came singing with a modish guitar!

Everyone there were astonished,

Our king in this avatar!

I swear not to believe my eyes;

Hello friends my dear subjects:

We are here to enjoy today,

Lets make today a memorable one:-

By forgetting our caste creed & religion is my say,

But recall that we always belong to this kingdom:-

But you are the king we are the subjects;

Lots of difference how can we ever forget that?

May be we are different creeds but how can you forget

That the universal language "Love"

doesnot belong to any one, any one caste, any creed:

Today atleast my subjects try to
understand the powers of love:-

A pat on the back, a kind smile on the face can make someone's
life a much better place!

Unity in diversity is all we need is all we want

With these final words the swans showered flowers from up
above and everyone dance with glee.

82. Dream so More!!!

Dream so more, dream so more my soul!!!!

Never end up upset and devasted in foul,

You are born to eat even the food roule;

Never in the mode of sully you be befoul

Initially winning every game is an afoul,

Such you grow & live outgrowing the ghoul;

Such you win every race oh legendary of prowl,

Excel well at preparations oh the soul so you there by becomes as time passes an oversoul!!!

Meaning:-

1. *Roule:- eatable Swiss roll*

2. *Befoul:- make dirty; pollute.*

3. *Afoul:- into conflict or difficulty with.*

4. *Ghoul:- an evil spirit or phantom, especially one supposed to rob graves and feed on dead bodies.*

5. *Prowl:- move about restlessly and stealthily, especially in search of prey.*

6. *Oversoul:- the absolute reality and basis of all existences conceived as a spiritual being in which the ideal nature imperfectly manifested in human beings is perfectly realized.*

83. Hidden Inner Voice!!!

A sudden score of voice from within burst out in support,

It could motivate anyone & everyone without any effort,

It was highly strong and bold, very fearless and cold!

It sang 'Say not I am fragile rather
increase energies by fire fold,

It was singing and dancing, a crazy yoga freak to the core!

It could foresee and forespeak into height it could soar,

But for learning its heart was yearning to know,
more, more and more;

It was my ruling lionize of loud thundering roar,

It was mighty and meditative in nature even in solitude,

Highly ecstatic and concerned about universal solicitude,

With a sharp eyesight & alertness, a guarding light, my soul!

It was very very brilliant and was rejoicing its status 'sole',

At times very clean, at times very dirty on the whole;

People stand in long long queues to get solutions
for their new questions was their goal,

Inspite of fame it was very simple in attire so,

But for terror and injustice it was a wild fiery soul;

Doing things of necessity to this entire universe
was its only prioritized goal!

Whole universe is at its feet which never
retires with a mode of bold,

The birth and death is at its one breath is all its real fact
but for hearts it just silently lavishly stole!!!

Meaning:-

1. *Solicitude:- care or concern for someone or something.*

2. *Solitude:- the state or situation of being alone.*

84. Motivational Thought

Simplicity in action & clarity at thought,

Are the major super lessons to be sought?

A fit body & a sharp intellect be all our aught,

Broadminded big thinks have already been taught,

Past days with foes of negation we have mightily fought,

And oceans of wisdom & knowledge let us at once waught,

Give the creative of creative innovative
ideas and spread endlessly the dought,

Give all the contribution to this
entire universe of forethought.

Spreading the cans & cans of positivity and fortune like a leader you lead and that you aren't a nought!

Meaning:-

1. *Thought:- an idea or opinion produced by thinking, or occurring suddenly in the mind.*

2. *Sought:- attempt or desire to obtain or achieve.*

3. *Aught:- anything at all, everything.*

4. *Waught:- to drink deeply.*

5. *Dought:- Virtue, positive ideals.*

6. *Fore thought:- careful consideration of what will be necessary or may happen in the future.*

7. *Nought:- Zero.*

85. It's a Brief Life!!!

You every day all spread the secret of youthfulness;
Forget that life is full of anger, anxiety & stressfulness,
Everyday wake up to renew the fresh new life of enjoyment!!!
Be adventurous & outgoing be not
circumspective in every moment!
Oh the joyful youth fill everyone
with bubbling & boiling enthusiasm,
Oh the captivating soul you arise as you
are born to become informative!
Share your wisdom & knowledge in a universal perspective;
Search the pathways of solutions for which you be inventive,
Come what may fix on all faces a big broad toothy smile,
With a gentle touch, heal all their pain & that
you are no more vain,
Be that humanitarian and leak your unlimited benevolence;
How long should mother nature be the giver of boons,
Enough you have borrowed from her
rather let us move on to serve,
Be a super solution to every problem as is time to heal,
Conscientious by nature be blemishless
in your every presence you steal;
And attract the all the audience with a positive deal,
Pacify all the ire and bring joy to all without tire,

Inspire to aspire oh the brilliant sharp intellect,

And let your exuberance out beat the pismire;

As you are born to achieve leave all the
clumsiness to the past,

A playful, whimsical & a waggish youth you
are meant to be alas,

A charming & cheerful heart is always
a blest soul isn't it not?

Be a colourful personality,
creative & unique with a votive heart;

Steal all the hearts with your bravery
Oh the master the informative mart,

Have a fit body with a healthy, sharp mind and
sweetness at heart is all your path!

Thus carefully climb the success ladder at par & remember
that you aren't a blind heart!!!

86. My Words Just for You

"You are totally born to do achieve" is my hearty adage

"But why err and say sorry later with a low voltage?"

"Ignite your light in twilight like a super sage"
"Just let your witty firmness speak all the age"
"Whatever you say, say it with high courage"

Oh my guide, the mentor, my intellect to you or
who else shall all I scream in rage,
By chasing away these negatives away you
outgrow from your disabled cage,

Question "how determined and steadfast is me in this life's
dramatic illusionary image?"

For all the negations do you know I have the perfect dosage!

Never be dissolved in this briny like mirage,

Enjoy every second in this life's entire voyage!

No one can calculate my sweet love for
this universe through any guage.

"Work for the wellbeing of this universe" is what my
mindlike front page says without discourage!!!

Meaning:-

1. Adage:- a proverb or short statement expressing a general
    truth.

2. Voltage:- pressure.

3. Sage:-wise, especially as.result of great experience.

4. Age:- a distinct period of history.

5.   Courage:- The quality of mind or spirit that enables a person to face difficulty, danger, pain, etc., without fear; bravery.

6.   Rage:- violent uncontrollable anger.

7.   Cage:-a structure of bars or wires in which birds or animals are confined.

8.   Image:- a representation of the external form of a person or thing in art.

9.   Dosage:- the size or frequency of a dose of a medicine or drug.

10. Mirage:- an unrealistic hope or wish that cannot be achieved.

11. Voyage:- a long journey involving travel by sea or in space.

12. Guage:-a measuring instrument.

13. Discourage:- cause (someone) to lose confidence or enthusiasm.

87. Hanuman the Burning Outfire!!!

The Ego exterminator comes boldly obliterating the ire,

In a mighty unique style, with a breath of fire;

Come what may even in-spite of dire,

He is patiently exuberant person even in-spite of tire;

In his every take, in-spite of situations of haywire,

He is the eradicator of hurdles busier than the pismire;

He is only my master Mr. Rudra who never expire,

"Oh the mighty destroyer" saying so I strongly admire;

"Inspire to aspire" saying so he flies beyond sky obliterating all the conspire!!!

Meaning:-

1. Ire:-Anger.

2. Fire:- a process in which substances combine chemically with oxygen from the air and typically give out bright light, heat, and smoke; combustion or burning.

3. Dire:-Extreamly serious or in urgency.

4. Tire:- feel or cause to feel in need of rest or sleep.

5. Haywire:- erratic; out of control.

6. Pismire:- an ant.

7. Expire:- come to the end of the period of validity.

8. Admire:- regard with respect or warm approval.

9. Conspire:- make secret plans jointly to commit an unlawful or harmful act.

88. Lessons to Seek!

When you welcome everyone to the realm of vivacity,

Don't give vague excuses and complain in absurdity,

With renewable energy you ignite the light in all of divinity,

Say not that I am a minority,
command respect with maturity,

You become that strong broadminded soul of nobility,

An incomparable but a steadfast person of generosity,

Realise & analise your true capacity & capability,

Become that virtuous person
who respects the entire humanity,

And carefully train and nurture oneself with super ability,

Dream & put into action by being a person of sagacity,

Fight out selfishness with your big think of generosity,

Just simply root out all the falsehood & vulgarity;

Life is also an impermanent circus so watch out with clarity,

Don't say I am hazy but obliterate
that you are a hopeless disability.

Meaning:-

1. *Vivacity:-* (especially in a woman) the quality of being attractively lively and animated.

2. *Absurdity:-* the quality or state of being ridiculous or wildly unreasonable.

3. *Divinity:-* the state or quality of being divine.

4. *Maturity:- the state, fact, or period of being mature.*

5. *Nobility:- the quality of being noble in character.*

6. *Generosity:- the quality of being kind and generous.*

7. *Capability:- the power or ability to do something.*

8. *Humanity:- the quality of being humane; benevolence.*

9. *Ability:- possession of the means or skill to do something.*

10. *Sagacity:- the quality of having or showing keen mental discernment and good judgement; wise or shrewd.*

11. *Vulgarity:- the state or quality of being vulgar.*

12. *Clarity:- the quality of being coherent and intelligible.*

13. *Disability:- the quality of being coherent and intelligible.*

89. A Strong Spiritual Appeal

Mesmerised I was by his strong spiritual appeal

Every work and every time he did with innate zeal

He was so engrossed in teach he totally forgot his meal

But still with everyone every time he signed a friendly deal

But for anytime and every-time he spread
on all the positive feel

When it comes for all positives you grab and selfishly steal

When it comes to devotion bow down to your
guru's pair of heel

He is a super master of innovative visions
and a super expert in self heal

90. Just Learn to

Honesty at action of unshakable will;

Confidence in eyes, beauty in character,

Exuberance at work of renewable perk;

Happiness in every act & holiness at heart,

Eliminate all the woes & defeat all the foes;

Crazy & craving to know more, more & more,

Show sincerity of conviction & purity of motive;

Possess gigantic intellect of high self-esteem at par,

Be that big industry of patience, love & innate peace;

And do remember to help the poor and needy at ease at ease.

91. Ingenuitified Inspiration

Hey do give a strong inspiration that is endless & limitless,

Say not that you are a worthless skint, you be fearless,

Stay courageous and don't stay meaningless;

You are born to help, not be helpless;

Serve the Ruth and the homeless,

Say not you are blind and ambitionless;

After all who you are to challenge the very boundless,

Spread your love universally & be not affectionless,

Understand your super strengths, why stay brainless,

You simply meditate be still & motionless,

Lots to learn in silence so stay bark less,

The almighty has gifted us so much with all the bless,

When you are feeling low look at the legless & armless,

Don't compare don't complaint say not you are comfortless,

With all the perky exuberance you never be cheerless,

When it comes to song sing easily breathless,

When it comes to feelings don't stay heartless;

Dignified be your action not mindless,

Such you succeed that you help the aimless;

Know the value of our parents from orphans the parentless,

*Be skillful & innovative not at all presume
that you are talentless;*

The very thought that you are a free bird is on so stay ageless,

Sing your soul's tunes melody not in the mode of rhythemless;

Be a performer no matter what not stay fruitless;

Be happy that your country is not leaderless!!!

Oh the eloquent speaker don't think that you are accent less?

*When your mighty & powerful why be scared &
think I am sightless?*

*Having consumed the food and salt of your
nation be loyal and not faithless,*

*Achievements are in your hands don't say and
think that you are worthless,*

*Give your selfless message to everyone & for
motivation you be endless.*

Meaning:-

1. Endless:- Never-ending.

2. Limitless:- without limit.

3. Skint:- (of a person) having little or no money available.

4. Meaningless:- without meaning.

5. Helpless:- unable to defend oneself or to act without help.

6. Homeless:- (of a person) without a home, and therefore typically living on the streets.

7. Ambitionless:- having no goal.

8. Boundless:- unlimited or immense.

9. Affectionless:- showing no affection or kindly disposition.

10. Brainless:- without intelligence.

11. Motionless:- without motion.

12. Accentless:- without proper accent.

13. Leaderless:- having no leader or no person in charge.

92. When Possibility is On!!!

Oh the motivational master you invigorate all,

Arise! inspite of plight, inspite of terrific downfall,

Come what may decimate the so-called complicated wall,

Such you inspire all that you be known
as an emboldening pal,

Once you reach to that great height,
you also grow spiritually tall,

Grab selfishly, when opportunities just simply knock and call,

Oh the motivating one!!! you enliven all;

Get going, get moving and intimate all;

Stay in the path of truth and such you fortify all,

The lessons of enlightenment you spread everyday to all,

Propel all the soaring visions and ignite soon the light in all;

That you are born to sweat for a great
cause and illuminate all,

Oh! you be known for innovative ideas
and lavishly spread among all;

You are just born to achieve and inspire all;
is the be all and end all.

Meaning:-

1. Invigorate:- Give strength or energy to.

2. Embolden:- give (someone) the courage or confidence to do
    something.

3.   Decimate:- kill, destroy, or remove a large proportion of.

4.   Fortify:- provide (a place) with defensive works as
     protection against attack.

5.   Enliven:- make (something) more entertaining, interesting,
     or appealing.

6.   Illuminate:- light up.

93. A Resonate Call

Master's deep thin voice resonates everyday all,

His soothing voice like melody alarms before I fall,

Where not is my master!!! Is the be all and the end all,

It is to Him that I bow down,
Oh! Hanuman you are my best pal;

You say "There is no right there is no wrong, its super master's
game overall,

Looking at all your selfless deeds,
people just enthrall and enthrall,

From nowhere you just appear just listening
to my hearty call;

Protector and savior of all, You outbeat the marshal,

Even before any menace befall,
You guard obliterating pitfall.

Meaning:-

1. *Appall:-* to overcome with consternation, shock, or dismay

2. *Befall:-* (especially of something bad) happen to (someone)

3. *Enthrall:-* Capture the fascinated attention of, Enslave.

4. *Marshal:-* An officer of the highest rank in the armed forces of some countries who guard their country.

94. Be a Fullfledged Wholehearted

Excuse mistakes oh the big hearted,
You are a free soul oh the free hearted;
Be a full hearted person not half hearted,
Teaching in every step you stay great hearted;
Never ever in sadness say I am broken hearted,
Inspite of committing mistakes you stay cold hearted;
Committing mistakes is not a crime oh the lion hearted,
Welcome all the nice hearted people so you be open hearted;
Such you spread joy to everyone oh the wholehearted!!!!
Be a giver of immense pleasure oh the sweet hearted,
Experiencing love at heart you stay soft hearted;
But for all achievements you stay proud hearted,
All your foes you obliterate oh the stonyhearted;
Why be stout hearted rather stay light hearted,
Don't ever lie rather forever stay true hearted;
Be strength giving machine not weak hearted.
Welcoming love from every corner of this
universe oh warm hearted.

95. You Be Such!!!

An ingenious, quick witted,
always on with an astute mindset,

Broadminded, high thinking, with an unfettered foresight;

An unwavering but a steadfast decision making insight;

Just, spreading a joyful contagious smile on every git,
even in every plight;

Why judge people right or wrong but seeing things as it is,
be your transparent sight,

Emboldening all of the needy with all the super strong might,

Forward planning, doing things of necessity
is you the Mr./Miss Bright,

You a ruler by choice, the super shining, my big beam of light.

Meaning:-

1. Ingenious:- (of a person) clever, original, and inventive.

2. Quick witted:- showing or characterized by an ability to think or respond quickly and effectively.

3. Astute:- having or showing an ability to accurately assess situations or people and turn this to one's advantage.

4. Broadminded:- tolerant or liberal in one's views and reactions; not easily offended.

5. Unfettered:- unrestrained or uninhibited.

6. Foresight:- the ability to predict what will happen or be needed in the future.

7. Unwavering:- not wavering; steady or resolute.

8. Contagious:- (of an emotion, feeling, or attitude) likely to spread to and affect others.

9. Plight:- a dangerous, difficult, or otherwise unfortunate situation.

10. Emboldening:- give (someone) the courage or confidence to do something.

96. "Words For You"

"Oh the towering intellect my enlightened one,

Give your eminent sanity of views to everyone;

Bring in that uncompromising truth in oneself my son,

You are my favourite, compassionate & hearty one,

Don't wait for but become that fullfledged one,

How sweet and passionate you are oh the dear one,

You are a luminous personality, oh the morally sublime one;

You are a person of super balance, oh my steadfast one,

You have been outdistancing the negative
distractions oh the dear one,

You never postpone things & love to be alone and alone,

Engrossed in meditative mindful prayers
into Samadhi you are prone,

Who else you are my own meditative master my own!!!"

No matter what happens you purify
me and my eternal entire zone!!!

Meaning:-

1. *Prone:- capable of*

2. *Fullfledged:- completely developed or established; fully fledged.*

3. *Sublime:- of very great excellence or beauty.*

4. *Eminent:- illustrious.*

5. Sanity:- the ability to think and behave in a normal and rational manner; sound mental health.

6. Steadfast:- Firm.

7. Towering:- extremely tall, especially in comparison with the surroundings.

97. Motivation

Root out the greed and dependency,

And master your linguistic profiency;

Growing nation strong with all the potency;

Spreading innovative ideas, be your own policy,

Being grammatically strong be your casual legacy,

Give creative of the creative ideologies with fluency,

Reverberate enthusiasm and utterly wipe out flouncy,

Do things cooly, not in sheer urgency,

Be open for learning by being pliancy,

By the way you expertise your cogency;

Spread and teach the values of "literacy",

Grow up quickly you are no more in infancy,

Everybody learns from mistakes and errancy,

Ignite every heart with luminous light of mercy-

Be the owner of solutions and lead with captaincy,

Reach out your answers to all but not in arrogancy,

With a balanced mindset; that is your hidden secrecy,

Before you die master and master oneself my ardency,

Oh! The ruler of the mind you be known for your decency,

Do the needful things, be intact; keep things in prudency,

Realise soon that you are unique not just normalcy,

Don't give space for an iota of selfishness and obduracy,

Outdistance all the negations such that you
be a big positive agency!!!

Throbbing and working to keep a fit body and mind; be your
mantra of buoyancy.

Meaning:-

1. *Flouncy: Go or move in an exaggeratedly impatient or angry manner.*

2. *Errancy: The condition of erring or straying from the accepted course or standards.*

3. *Pliancy: Easily bent, flexible.*

4. *Cogency: The quality of being clear, logical, and convincing; lucidity.*

5. *Ardency: Very enthusiastic or passionate, Burning; glowing.*

6. *Prudency: careful and avoiding risks*

7. *Buoyancy: success and a lot of activity in an economy, market, etc.*

8. *Normalcy: being normal*

9. *Obduracy: Stubbornly refusing to change one's opinion or course of action*

10. *Captaincy: The position or period of command over a team, ship, or aircraft.*

11. *Luminous: Giving off light; bright or shining.*

98. Bharat Mata

A super melody queen out-bursting in holiness,

Within experiencing high exalted consciousness-

Singing omkar every time in silence of loudness;

She always sat in unmoving & in extreme stillness,

Who else she is the mother of prosperity & richness;

My most affectionate mother full of perk & liveliness,

This philanthropic mother was gentle known for helpfulness;

Popularly this mother was known
for graceful dance & fitness,

Selfless reverberation starts if she starts
singings shambo in firmness;

Super eloquent writer & speaker is my powerful
mother of mightiness;

A holistically a strong lady with a poetic
firmament my clever mother of smartness;

A super poetize, amazing author known
for creativity & innovativeness,

She invests passion in every action obliterating
dullness and darkness,

Very famously known for cleanliness,
cleverness & playfulness;

Her full life is a seek & inspiration of eternal cheerfulness,

Her every do is full of involvement & mindfulness;

Full of gratitude to her master shambo in devotedness,

Engrossed in meditative mode is my mother gentleness;

*She a famous lady for goodness, richness & cleverness who
is indeed my true madness!!!*

99. Mother Sharada

Highly famous for singing is my daring mother glory,

Let it be any difficult situation she is not an arbitrary;

For ages together, she is very famous as a dictionary,

Always in a meditative mode she loves to be solitary;

Highly brilliant in nature, she is truly extraordinary,

She rules the entire cosmos without any adversary;

Mother cosmos inspires everyone in the mode of a visionary,

Mute by nature, look at her stature,
she herself is a big library,

Commanding respect in every path,
she is herself an honorary;

Ask any question in no time there are super
solutions of great vocabulary;

She says respect time as its prime and do things
that are highly necessary,

Super innovative ideas roll down her tongue,
she is all our beneficiary;

Balancing herself on the tip of the fame
she serves and gaurds voluntary,

She gifts the super traits to all,
she herself is our precious gift of complementary,
This gracious and benevolent mother
is a philianthrophic is all the summary,

For a single problem varieties of solutions, ruling the entire
universe in the mode of proprietary;

A queen by chance, catalyst by choice, a universal teacher,
her entire life is a disciplined itenary.

Meaning:-

1. *Glory:- a great admiration, honour, and praise that you earn by doing something successfully.*

2. *Arbitrary:- unrestrained and autocratic in the use of authority.*

3. *Dictionary:- a book or electronic resource that lists the words of a language (typically in alphabetical order) and gives their meaning, or gives the equivalent words in a different language, often also providing information about pronunciation, origin, and usage.*

4. *Solitary:- saddened by isolation.*

5. *Extraordinary:- very unusual or remarkable.*

6. *Adversary:- Enemy.*

7. *Visionary:- someone with a strong vision of the future.*

8. *Honarary:- conferred as an honour, without the usual requirements or functions.*

9. *Library:- a building or room containing collections of books, periodicals, and sometimes films and recorded music for use or borrowing by the public or the members of an institution.*

10. *Vocabulary:- the body of words used in a particular language.*

11. *Beneficiary:- a person who derives advantage from something, especially a trust, will, or life insurance policy.*

12. *Summary:- a brief statement or account of the main points of something.*

13. *Proprietary:- one that possesses, owns, or holds exclusive right to something.*

14. *Voluntary:- done, given, or acting of one's own free will.*

15. *Complimentary:- gift given or supplied free of charge.*

16. *Catalyst:- a person or thing that precipitates an event.*

17. *Itenary:- the route of a journey.*

100. Learn

A new surge of hope just coruscated in motion!

Eratically it started dancing & screaming in ovation;

"Unleash your creativity" it said and kept
on singing in elation,

It said "Radiate exuberance in every action
& highlight your passion",

Think that you are a universal citizen,
living in God gifted mansion,

But for worship and devotion your heart is the best option,

Do puncture your ego and desire, it is but a steadfast caution,

For every difficult question from within
do find the super solution,

Increase the eruption of innovative ideas let it
flow like volcano of ocean,

Ignite your inner fire of commitment and prioritisation,

In-spite of the impermanent circus of life,
you be full of action,

With all the adventure and determination
you hied towards focalisation.

Meaning:-

1. Motion:- the action or process of moving or being moved.

2. Elation:- great happiness and exhilaration.

3. *Ovation:- a sustained and enthusiastic show of appreciation from an audience, especially by means of applause.*

4. *Passion:- strong and barely controllable emotion.*

5. *Mansion:- a large, impressive house.*

6. *Option:- a thing that is or may be chosen.*

7. *Caution:- care taken to avoid danger or mistakes.*

8. *Solution:- a means of solving a problem or dealing with a difficult situation.*

9. *Ocean:- Larger sea.*

10. *Prioritisation:- the action or process of deciding the relative importance or urgency of a thing or things.*

11. *Action:- Enthusiasm.*

12. *Determination:- the quality of being determined; firmness of purpose.*

13. *Focalisation:- the act of bringing into focus.*

About the Author

Dear all readers, i am Priyamvada one of kruti's favourite teachers in her life. I m a lecturer at Auden school hoskerehalli. I am a wellwisher of kruti. I say this because all her age group girls used get married and settle in life, but this girl caught my attention as she was flexibly writing. I am inspired as she used to show me her writings to avoid grammatical mistakes. I have truely enjoyed reading her poetry as a teacher I am also a fan of kruti now. One unique thing is most of her poetry are Rhyming and full of morals and virtues. She was so engrossed in writing she did not want to work but write. But it was I who inspired her to take up a job as its nothing more than becoming economically independent as no one were ready to fund her poetry book as being writer without job is a shame and wont have respect for writings. It was I who motivated to take up a job. And for godsake she is working now in Wellsfargo an American bank as an Intern analyst in bengaluru. I m very happy to have found such a passionate writer and orator. From her school days she was good in debates and oratory. I am proud to have her as my student. Let god bless her forever. By Priyamvada.